Wisconsin
The Way We Were

Wisconsin
The Way We Were

by
Mary A. Shafer

Heartland Press
An imprint of NorthWord Press, Inc.
P.O. Box 1360 • Minocqua, WI 54548

Wisconsin
The Way We Were

Text and captions copyright © 1993 Mary A. Shafer
Photos copyright credited institutions

Designed by The Art Emporium
Park Falls, WI

Printed in U.S.A.

Edited by Greg Linder

Published by Heartland Press
An imprint of NorthWord Press, Inc.
P.O. Box 1360 • Minocqua WI 54548

For a free color catalog of Heartland/NorthWord
nature books and gifts, call 1-800-336-5666.

Library of Congress Cataloging In Publication Data

Shafer, Mary A.
  Wisconsin: the way we were, 1845-1945 / by Mary A. Shafer.
      p.   cm.
    ISBN 1-55971-156-6 : $19.95
    1. Wisconsin—History.   I. Title.
F581.S53 1993
977.4'04—dc20   92-42347
                                            CIP

Wisconsin: **The Way We Were** is dedicated to my beloved grandmother, Alice Downer Shafer, whose passing during the writing of this book precluded her seeing it published. Her stories taught me to love words and the human drama of history. Her devotion and unwavering support have made my most significant accomplishments possible and worthwhile, and her belief in me made me believe in myself. She was my hero and my friend.

Contents

Photo Courtesy Ralph Weblitz

Badger Profiles

Acknowledgments

First of all, I want to thank my family for their interest in and support of my work. Specifically, I'd like to thank my sister and future journalist Rebecca Valentine for her generosity with her time. She gave the original draft its first read-through and offered countless other suggestions in the midst of classes, family crisis and carrying a baby.

I wouldn't have become as interested as I am in Wisconsin history were it not for the inspiration and guidance of my partner, Susan Cook, whose rich personal library proved a great resource for this project. I'd like also to thank her grandmother, Irene Kostrzewa, for taking the time to talk with me about her experiences as a lifelong Wisconsin resident.

Certain others must be mentioned who took the time to help me develop my abilities: Sheryl Van Haren, hero and mentor (whether she knows it or not); Gerry Laine, mind-opener extraordinaire; Chris Hansen, enthusiastic teacher, kind friend and integrity personified.

Moral support was provided by all of the above and a few good friends who stood by cheering over the long haul: Jan and Gene D'Alessandro, Cindy V, Jen Porter, Deanna Braaten and "Goo."

Nancy Cavanaugh went above and beyond the call of duty as technical advisor, bringing me kicking and screaming into the computer age.

Invaluable research help was provided by: Diane Peterson, Marathon County Public Library, who pointed me in the right direction; Mary Jane Hettinga, Marathon County Historical Society, who endured many afternoons of my ransacking her collections; Dave Rogers, who cheerfully and enthusiastically provided information and photographs from the J.I. Case Company archives; Joannie Kloster, whose knowledge of her charges in the library at the Manitowoc Maritime Museum was impressive and made my research there a joy; Mr. Roland Applin, who took the time to write a personal account of his years with the CCC and generously lent personal photos; Evelyn Lee, who took me on a personal tour through Woodruff's Dr. Kate Museum; Mr. Donn Holder, Jackson County Historical Society; Richard Beggs, Clintonville Area Historical Society; Jean Houston of Al Capone's Hideaway; Jean D. Reese, H.H. Bennett Studio Foundation; Judith Simonsen, Milwaukee County Historical Society; George Miller, Ripon College; Lorraine Lindell, Laura Ingalls Wilder Memorial Society; Cindy Knight, archivist at the State Historical Society of Wisconsin, and countless librarians throughout the state.

And of course I must thank Greg Linder, who has been a firm but gentle editor and a real pal.

Foreword

You might justifiably ask yourself: "Why another book on Wisconsin? Hasn't everything we want to know about our beautiful state been written by now?"

In a word, no.

Certainly the "important" dates, events, and celebrities have been covered time and again. Wisconsin politics, economics, wars, and technologies have been reported on *ad infinitum*. But the countless academic treatments of Wisconsin's history have often neglected the force behind all events and situations . . . people.

People made the events happen, lived through them, suffered their consequences, and at times prospered from them. *Wisconsin: The Way We Were* is primarily about people. It reflects the belief that dates and events are important only insofar as they affect the people involved, and that "history" is really "ourstory."

So we'll focus on the folks who made the Badger State the unique place that it is—a microcosm of America with its own idiosyncrasies, its own heroes and villains, and its own past. Places, events, and dates are here, but they serve mostly as a backdrop for the human drama that unfolded as one state grew up.

I invite you to sift with me through the pages of Wisconsin's past.

Mary A. Shafer
Springstead, Wisconsin

A lumber camp cook and cookee clean up the dinner dishes aboard a wanigan, a floating kitchen raft used on logging river runs, in this 1886 photo by H. H. Bennett.

Chapter One

BUSTING SOD

"Meskousing" was the name given by guides from the Upper Fox River Valley tribes to the river that flowed through the area now known as Portage. One of their employers, Jesuit priest Louis Joliet, recorded the name as "Miskonsing" in the journal of his explorations. Joliet's successor, another black robe named Louis Hennepin, gave the name a French twist by changing it to "Ouisconsin," derived from the Algonquin word meaning "muskrat hole."

During the entire French regime, this great river lent its name to the vast amount of territory through which it flowed. When the territory was ceded to England by the Treaty of Paris in 1763, the name was anglicized to "Wisconsin."

By 1845, Wisconsin's early reign as a hotbed of French and English fur trading was over. Its original inhabitants, the Native Americans, were all but gone, and those who remained were confined to reservations after the turning point of the Black Hawk Wars. Statehood was just three years away for the bustling territory, which formed one of the farthest western boundaries of America's settlement frontier. Vast veins of lead ore, discovered close to the surface, had given birth to mining boomtowns in the southwest region along the Mississippi River.

The Mississippi had become a main transportation route for goods and services. Up the river to the lumber towns of Wisconsin's sprawling timberlands came barges loaded with grain and other food staples, weapons and ammunition, yard goods, and even culture in the form of musical instruments and printing presses. Passing these barges and steamers in the opposite direction were legions of "timber monkeys" astride half-submerged logs, using spiked levers called peaveys to shepherd the great flotillas to southern mills. The logs would ultimately become building materials for rapidly growing industrial cities like Milwaukee, Racine, and Kenosha. Some logs made it as far south as St. Louis.

In 1847, Knapp, Stout and Company purchased thousands of wooded acres south of current-day Chetek from the government at $1.25 each. Logging began in Barron County the following year, establishing mill towns such as Menomonie, and by 1870 the firm was the largest lumber corporation in the world. In its immense zeal to turn gigantic profits, the company soon exhausted the area's supply of white pine. In 1901, the KS & C mills shut down.

Charles Q. Eldredge, a New England native, traveled to the pine forest to make his fortune with a similar outfit, and found that being a lumberjack was both difficult and dangerous. His memoirs describe his arrival at his first lumber camp in Werner, 12 miles north of New London:

> I wore the boots that I had brought from Connecticut and the second day out my feet and legs, to nearly my knees, were frozen badly. My boots were cut off, my feet and my legs were soaked in kerosene oil. In a few days I could get around, but it was many years before I ever attempted to wear a boot. Moccasins in that climate were necessary, for unless the joints work, the foot will freeze.

Der Neue stählerne Deering Junior Binder mit stählernem
Garbenträger an der Arbeit im Felde.

This 1840s engraving shows a horse-drawn hay thresher/binder manufactured by Deering. It incorporated the Appleby-designed twine binder, mounted on the driver's right.

I worked that winter as a "swamper," did a man's work and kept my eyes open. We lived on salt beef, salt pork, beans, hot wheat bread every meal, tea and sorghum molasses. No vegetables, no coffee, no sugar, no butter. Men went out to work in the morning while the stars still shone and never came in till they saw them again, except for a thirty-minute stop for dinner. No card playing was allowed, and no talking after nine o'clock. My first winter in the woods is remarkable in looking back upon it for just one thing; that I really survived it.

Central areas of the rolling Kettle Moraine were rich with dark alluvial soil, a legacy of the ancient glaciers that plowed through the region on their way to the Great Lakes basin. Farmers flocked here by the thousands to take advantage of the agriculturally fertile conditions.

Madison sat on the edge of the "driftless" area, part of the territory that was left untouched by the glaciers. During a lively 42-day session of the first territorial legislature nearly a decade earlier, in anticipation of Wisconsin's admission to statehood, the city had been chosen as the site of a permanent state capitol.

Railroads first appeared as inroads to the northern timber stands. They were an efficient means of getting the lumber to market. The simple days of horse and buggy travel would never be the same after the introduction of the shining, parallel rails and the steam-driven, smoke-belching chariots that flew along them like greased lightning–at that time, about 15 miles per hour.

As ever, there was nature to contend with. Homesteaders found themselves confronted with every kind of problem from drought and famine to flood, fire, and violent storms. Infestations of locusts, tent caterpillars, and other pests stripped crops and devastated other vegetation. In the north, slash piles left by the lumbering operations were wildfires waiting to happen.

Long Day's Journey

Sometimes, just getting to the place they would call "home" was enough to try the nerves of even the most dedicated settlers. Before the railroads branched out to serve the general public, overland travel was mostly a matter of riding in some horse- or ox-drawn conveyance. Those without even these primitive vehicles resorted to the cheapest and most accessible of all modes of travel–walking.

Often, travel on foot was necessary for at least some part of a trip, after the adventurers had gone as far as wagon roads and boats could take them. The majority of these travelers had with them everything they owned in the world, including furniture,

Larry Mishkar Collection

The Wisconsin Central Railway constructs a steel girder bridge, extending its track in the 1880s.

A growing farmstead: Wisconsin settlers at home prior to 1900.

livestock, cooking utensils (usually made of iron), and other heavy items. Moving to Wisconsin was an enormous task.

Much of our insight into settlement comes from the diaries of pioneer women. One such woman, Juliette Kinzie, wrote an account of her horseback ride from Portage to Chicago in the early 1830s. Stopping near the site of present-day Madison to set up their tent for the night, her party changed into sleeping attire. Kinzie had hung her riding habit over the end of a log. According to her journal, it was so cold that her clothing was "in a very few minutes, frozen so stiff as to stand upright, giving the appearance of a dress out of which a lady has vanished."

Other pioneers had similar experiences at the hands of Mother Nature. The following account concerns the 1837 arrival of Rosaline Peck, her husband Eben, and their two-year-old son. They were the first white settlers in Madison, having left their tavern business behind in Blue Mound, 25 miles to the west:

> We pitched our tent . . . within three miles of Madison; rested comfortably till near 3 o'clock on Saturday morning, when we were awakened by a tremendous wind storm, and howling of wolves, and found snow five or six inches deep which continued to fall until after we arrived in Madison. Well, now, here we are at Madison . . . sitting in a wagon under a tree, with a bed-quilt thrown over my own and my little boy's heads, in a tremendous storm of snow and sleet, twenty-five miles from inhabitants on one side and nearly one hundred on the other.

There are two precious words that the Peck family might not have fully appreciated on that cold, stormy evening: *Welcome home.*

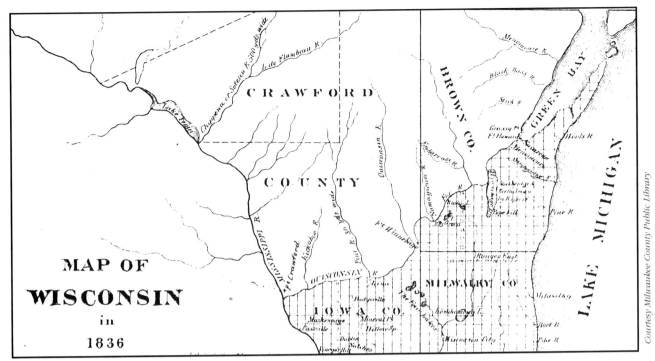

This map from Increase Lapham's "Geography of Wisconsin" shows the territory as it existed in 1836.

Making It Official

By 1848, Wisconsin Territory's population had grown enough to allow it to petition for statehood. Lead mining was in its heyday near Mineral Point, and settlers had established a strong agricultural foothold. Henry Dodge and James Doty had been playing musical chairs with the governor's seat for years, and the two main political parties were the Democrats and Whigs.

On May 29, 1848, President Polk signed legislation creating the state of Wisconsin, 30th state to join the Union, itself less than 75 years old.

Congress didn't pass the Homestead Act until 1862, but southern Wisconsin was being settled well before that time. As major centers of commerce and transportation connections such as Mineral Point, Milwaukee, and Kenosha began to become metropolitan areas, new residents began settling farther inland from the lakes and rivers that bordered the state.

Many of the earliest settlers came from Europe. Most were of hardy farming stock and had come to carry on their traditions in the New World. They were looking for the wide open spaces they had heard so much about, vast acreages that could produce enough grain to feed their stock, and they were rarely disappointed.

Much of the unclaimed land lay in the cutover areas of the north, now denuded of trees and available for a song, since the lumber companies viewed the land as an expensive liability. Jens Rasmussen, the first permanent farmer in Rosholt, south of Wausau, came to his land in 1867. Land was going for about $1.25 per acre. Three years later Rasmussen's land–35 cleared acres, five wooded acres, and 40 unimproved acres–was valued at $1,000. The census that year recorded his stock of two dairy cows, four oxen, three beef cattle, and two hogs at a total value of $300.

At times, the expansiveness of the land exceeded even the grandest expectations. Some new settlers were overwhelmed by the rolling moraines covered with native grasses that were taller than a person. Linka Preus, a Lutheran pastor's wife, wrote in 1851 that the wind rippling in waves across these golden prairie gras-ses made the landscape look like "the wild billowing sea."

The first portable steam engine rolled out of the J.I. Case shop in 1869, more than 15 years ahead of the real boom in farm steam engine use. This horse-drawn machine churned out approximately 8 to 10 horsepower and burned wood, coal, or straw in its boiler. J.I. Case manufactured more steam engines and threshing machines than any other company in history.

Soon, however, settlers learned to appreciate the generosity of soil that could give birth to such thick, sturdy growth, and wanted to share their good fortune. After it was too dark to do chores outside, they wrote long and sometimes lonely letters in the dim, flickering light of kerosene lanterns to their families back in the Old Country. They often sang the praises of the cheap, fertile land of their adopted home, hoping to entice their relatives to join them.

From her home in Spring Prairie, Preus reported to her parents in an 1852 letter:

> Today I made a discovery which shows how luxuriant vegetation is in America. My kitchen table consists of a box we brought from Norway. This we inverted and provided with four legs, beautifully turned and polished by nature herself, from a poplar tree growing in the woods just outside our door. To be sure, they were frozen and raw, but what of it? That only contributes to the vigor of the growth.

> To my great delight, I discovered that the legs have been sprouting lovely green side branches, covered with green leaves. One of the green shoots I shall enclose in a letter to Norway–it has grown on my kitchen table!

Where There's a Will . . .

Despite the hardiness of Wisconsin's soil, farm life had its attendant hardships. But the challenges were met by the new farmers with the same progressive optimism that had led them to load their wagons and head West in the first place. Many entrepreneurs used Wisconsin farmland as a proving ground for their inventions.

Cyrus McCormick of Virginia patented a reaper in 1834. His machine mowed stalks while a man raked off the grain on a rear-mounted platform. Nearly one-tenth of the 1500 machines manufactured after 1846 were sold in Wisconsin, replacing the cradle and scythe-by-hand methods.

Wisconsin's own John Appleby of La Grange came up with the first viable twine binder during the Civil War years, a device that made the baling of cut hay and other grasses easier and more efficient.

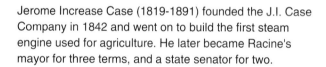

Jerome Increase Case (1819-1891) founded the J.I. Case Company in 1842 and went on to build the first steam engine used for agriculture. He later became Racine's mayor for three terms, and a state senator for two.

Experimentation with prototypes took him to Beloit and Mazomanie, although the twine binder was eventually manufactured in Virginia by McCormick, who bought the rights. Appleby went on to sell the original manufacturing plant where he invented the binder, thereby laying the foundation for what would become the International Harvester Company.

Another major equipment manufacturer got its start in Wisconsin and remains a prominent state business entity. In 1844, Jerome Increase Case demonstrated his new threshing machine in Rochester, Wisconsin. The machine not only stripped grain from the stalks, but also separated the chaff, performing two previously distinct operations. Power was provided by horses on a treadmill, and the contraption sold for $300. Steam later powered these machines, and engines and tractors eventually became part of Case's heavy equipment line.

Milwaukee's elegant Newhall House hotel, built in 1857 at the corner of Broadway and Michigan, was the accommodation of choice of many celebrities and dignitaries. The hotel was completely destroyed by fire on January 10, 1883.

One of the major obstacles to tillage in the northern half of the state was the prevalence of stumps left behind by loggers as they passed through. All stumps had to be removed before the soil could be broken by a plow, and anyone who has ever seen the massive root network of a tree can imagine the work that went into each of these stump routings. Sometimes it took an entire season to clear a field of stumps and rocks, leaving the farmer with no time to plant before the onset of winter. The dilemma was tackled head-on by farmers, who devised many methods to remove stumps–from blasting with dynamite to erecting tall, tripod-like "stump screws" to pull them out.

The Price of Progress

Stumps weren't the only nuisance left behind by the logging operations. Enormous piles of "slash"—branches, limbs, and foliage removed from felled trees—were left in the cutovers to rot. These heaps became tinder for intermittent fires that raged throughout the northwoods for decades.

During the Civil War, as Ulysses Grant led the Army of the Potomac against Robert E. Lee's Army of Northern Virginia in the siege of Petersburg, a great conflagration surrounded the lumber town of Wausau, destroying several sawmills, homes, and barns. It was an early example of the damage that careless forest management can cause. The town's entire population fought the flames and saved most of their homes. It's a measure of the isolation of northern Wisconsin at the time that only local and regional newspapers mentioned this great blaze.

In 1863, a wildfire of unknown origin on Lake Superior's southwestern shore produced such thick smoke that it blacked out the sun for days, polluting the air as far south as Milwaukee. A year later, a severe drought had turned the northwoods into a tinderbox. Small fires of the common springtime variety, usually started by lightning or sparks from a train, spread over larger areas and became more numerous. Fed by the dry conditions, they spread as far south as Two Rivers in the east and Neillsville in the west.

Not all fires were caused by leftovers from the lumber trade. Carelessness was the cause of a fire that swept through Spencer in August of 1886, consuming a lumber mill, several barns, homes, and a boarding house. A man named Cressy lost control of a fire he had started (probably to burn trash) on his property just west of town. For days, the fire burned on the outskirts of Spencer, kept at bay by favorable winds. Then, on August 7, the winds abruptly changed direction and blew the flames toward town.

Despite the efforts of many men to fight the blaze before it could engulf the mill yard, the flames spread into the center of town, fed by the lumber at the mill. The heat was so intense that it warped the train rails and burned down the water tower at the depot, despite its liquid contents. People hastily loaded wagons with household belongings, carted them across town, unloaded the wagons, and headed back for more. This saved many possessions that would otherwise have been lost, but in the end, nearly half the town was destroyed.

One particularly tragic fire occurred in Milwaukee. Since it opened in 1857, the elegant Newhall House hotel had attracted traveling dignitaries and celebrities. On January 10, 1883, a fire of unknown origin engulfed the entire building. Although most patrons escaped, over 70 people weren't so lucky. Many of those who did manage to escape the flames died when they jumped from windows, bounced off telegraph wires below, and were dashed against the building.

At the other end of the disaster scale are floods, and Wisconsin has had its share. In July of 1911, heavy rains caused the Black River to rise and wash out the western embankment of the Dells dam, above a smaller dam at Hatfield. Despite efforts to strengthen it, the Dells dam let go again on October 6, this time taking the Hatfield embankment with it. By noon that day, angry water swirled about the pilings of the railroad bridge in Black River Falls.

Courtesy Black River Falls Historical Society

Even buildings as far as three blocks from the main channel weren't safe from the raging torrents of the 1911 Black River flood.

Railroad cars are awash in the flood waters of the Wisconsin River. The photograph was taken in Wausau on July 24, 1912.

Larry Mishkar Collection

Residents were ordered off the streets just as the water breached the new dam wall. Bridges, frame buildings, and assorted smaller debris were washed away in the rampaging waves, while several large brick buildings toppled in the onslaught of the powerful current. In the end, the flood destroyed nearly 80 buildings in the downtown area, damaged 20 more, and caused an estimated $2 million in damage–a true catastrophe in those times. More than 200 people found themselves unemployed while their workplaces were rebuilt.

Here are listings excerpted from a published accounting of losses due to the Black River flood:

- William Quimbach, Tin Shop–household goods and piano, nothing saved but clothing on back . . . $1700

- John Marsh & Son–brick store building and stock of dry goods. Decline to give estimate, but it will rank among the big ones.

- Dr. H. Kalling–X-ray machine and some medicines and office furniture . . .$600.

The Peshtigo Fire

A bird's-eye view of Peshtigo as it existed before the great fire in 1871.

Courtesy Peshtigo Fire Museum

Arguably the worst disaster in Wisconsin history came about through ignorance and thoughtlessness. The Peshtigo Fire occurred on October 8, 1871, encompassing four counties surrounding the city of Green Bay. Much of the damage from this great fire could have been avoided.

The year had been an especially dry one, and farmers took advantage of the lack of rain to clear more land by cutting and burning woodlots. A company of laborers used the same method to clear more right-of-way for the railbed they were laying through the area. Hunters and Indians who spent time in the woods cooked with fire, and burned wood to keep wild animals at bay while they slept.

The one thing all these people had in common was their failure to safely extinguish the fires. When traveling through the region that fall, it was common to see many small fires flickering across the forest floor, consuming leaf litter,

fallen branches, and other flammable debris.

In previous weeks, several small but dangerous fires had made the residents of the Peshtigo area nervous enough to set buckets of water outside of their homes, but they took no other measures to prevent wildfires.

By about 8:30 on the evening of October 8th, a dense cloud of smoke with crimson reflections beneath it was visible from the middle of Peshtigo, near a spot where the river forks off into a small stream. This ominous sight was accompanied by a mysterious, low rumbling, like continuously rolling thunder. A strong wind had arisen and was surging ahead of the flames, a vanguard of the terrible destruction to come.

When the terrified townsfolk finally realized what was happening, they rushed en masse toward the river. Others rushed about willy-nilly, hysterical and without direction. Many

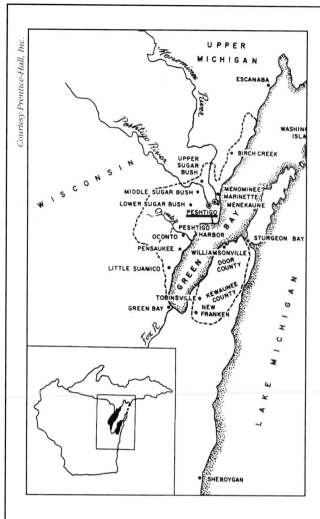

The dotted lines on this map indicate the portion of Wisconsin that was devastated by the Peshtigo fire.

as far as the eye could reach were covered with people standing there, motionless as statues, some with eyes staring, upturned towards heaven, and tongues protruded. The greater number seemed to have no idea of taking any steps to procure their safety, imagining, as many afterwards acknowledged to me, that the end of the world had arrived and that there was nothing for them but silent submission to their fate.

Without uttering a word—the violence of the storm entirely precluded anything like speech—I pushed the persons standing on each side of me into the water. One of these sprang back again with a half-smothered cry . . . but immersion in water is better than immersion in fire. I caught him again and dragged him out with me into the river as far as possible. At the same moment I heard a splash of water along the river's brink. All had followed my example.

young men who had arrived the previous night to work on the railroad lay about in drunken stupors from a full day of revelry in the tavern. As the main body of the fire approached, the wind became even more violent, throwing people and objects down ahead of it.

Amidst a whirl of smoke at the riverside, dust and cinders rendered the air almost impossible to breathe. People swirled about in mass confusion. Father Peter Pepin, whose personal account of his survival of the fire is the most complete in existence, led the way into the water, perceiving the river as the only means of salvation from the blaze. He details his horrific experience:

The whirlwind in its continual ascension had, so to speak, worked up the smoke, dust, and cinders, so that at least we could see clear before us. The banks of the river

Those who weren't paralyzed by terror followed Father Pepin into the current. Flames leapt over the river; gases burned in the supercharged air. People ducked under the water, protecting their necessarily exposed heads by splashing water over them or by covering their heads with soaked quilts and blankets. After almost five hours of submersion in the river while the firestorm raged all around, those who hadn't drowned staggered onto the banks. The sands were still warm from the scorching they had received.

In all, the fire consumed over 1,150 square miles of standing timber and farmland, covering most of Door County and large areas of Oconto, Brown, and Kewaunee counties. Estimates of the immediate dead ranged between 1,200 and 1,500, not including those who subsequently died from burns or other wounds inflicted by the fire.

In a horrifying coincidence, the city of Chicago, far to the south, burned on that same night, the flames there fanned by the same southwest wind. Due to the extreme isolation of the Peshtigo area, the outside world did not learn of the great wildfire there until two days later. Meanwhile, most of the trains and other means of transportation in downstate Wisconsin were dedicated to a relief effort for victims of the Chicago fire. In fact, Wisconsin Governor Lucius Fairchild, along with top aides, had accompanied trainloads of emergency supplies to Illinois.

When a telegram reporting the Peshtigo disaster was received at the capitol on the morning of October 10, Mrs. Fairchild took charge and became, for all practical purposes, governor in her husband's absence. She commandeered a boxcar loaded with supplies that was originally destined for Chicago, rallied Madison women who put blankets in the already-stuffed car for protection against the autumn chill, ordered railroad officials to give the boxcar priority over other traffic, and sent it on its way north. After that train left, Mrs. Fairchild appealed to the public for donations of money, clothing, and other emergency goods. The response to her request was so overwhelming that a second fully filled boxcar left for Peshtigo that same night.

Hardship and turmoil bring out the best and the worst in people. In this respect, Wisconsin is no different than any other state or country. But an indication of the supple fiber of Wisconsin's people is found in the words of Governor Cadwallader Washburn, who traveled to the ravaged region just over a year after the fire had swept through. He wrote:

> I visited the burnt district on the peninsula, [and] the west side of Green Bay. I found the devastation produced by the fire fiend such as is impossible for the mind to comprehend without the aid of the eye. I was pleased to find that a majority of the survivors had returned to their clearings; many had raised fair crops, and were hopeful of the future . . .

BADGER PROFILE: From Little House to Libraries

Laura Ingalls Wilder
1867-1957

The mush was gone. Pa scraped the last drop of milk from his bowl and drank his tea. "Well," he said, "we can't have a tree, for there isn't so much as a bush on Silver Lake. We wouldn't want one anyway, just for ourselves. But we can have a little Sunday-school celebration of our own, Mary."

He went to get his fiddle box, and while Ma and Laura washed the bowls and the pot and set them away, he tuned the fiddle and rosined the bow.

Frost was thick on the windowpanes and frost furred the cracks around the door. Thickly against the clear upper edges of the windowpanes the snowflakes fluttered. But lamplight was bright on the red-and-white tablecloth, and the fire glowed behind the open drafts of the stove.

–From *On The Shores of Silver Lake*

At the age of 63, Laura Ingalls Wilder was encouraged by her daughter to write about her life as a pioneer child on the Wisconsin plains. The resulting seven volumes, referred to as the "Little House" books, have become classics in children's literature. Although somewhat fictionalized, they are highly autobiographical, telling the story of Wilder's life from the time of her fourth year through her marriage to Almanzo Wilder in 1885, when she was 18.

Laura's story begins on a homestead in Pepin County, Wisconsin, where she was born. The first book of the series, *Little House in the Big Woods,* describes her life in the family's log cabin. The remaining volumes detail the family's move across the Mississippi to Indian lands in Kansas territory, where they were forced by the government to leave their homestead; life in Minnesota, where Laura first entered school; the family's life in a railroad camp and the establishment of the town of De Smet, South Dakota; the severe winter of 1881 in De Smet; Laura's adolescent years and the end of her high school career when she became a teacher at age 15; and her teaching life, courtship, and marriage.

Wilder received a special recognition at the 1954 Newbery-Caldecott dinner, and the Children's Library Association honored her by establishing the Laura Ingalls Wilder Award, of which she was the first recipient. Her books have remained popular with children and adults, and they also inspired a long-running television series, *Little House on the Prairie.*

A historical marker located on Wisconsin state highway 35 in Pepin Park reveals the author's surprise at her own success. After publication of her first book, she thought:

> . . . that would end it. But what do you think? Children who read it wrote me begging for more. I was amazed because I didn't know how to write. I went to little red schoolhouses all over the West and I never graduated from anything.

Laura Ingalls Wilder died in 1957, leaving a legacy of memories and experiences from an age that might otherwise have been forgotten.

BADGER PROFILE: A Man for All Seasons

One of 13 children born to Seneca Lapham in Palmyra, New York, Increase A. Lapham followed his father into the business of canal building. Seneca had worked on the Erie Canal, and by the time Increase was 15 years old, he also became a laborer on the Ohio River Falls branch of the same project.

During his digging, Increase cracked open a stone to reveal a cache of fossils, and immediately became fascinated with the study of antiquities. He began a collection of dried plants for an herbarium, which eventually included over 8,000 specimens.

At 24, Lapham arrived in Milwaukee to become chief engineer and secretary of Byron Kilbourn's Rock River Canal Company. Serving also as Register of Claims for the city, he began mapping Indian burial mounds, some of which had been damaged or destroyed by new home-building.

Born with a keen sense of curiosity, Lapham schooled himself in botany, meteorology, geology, archaeology, zoology, and horticulture. In 1836, he wrote the first scientific imprint in the Northwest territories, his *Catalogue of Plants and Shells Found in the Vicinity of Milwaukee.* The first book published in the state was his *Geographical and Topographical Description of Wisconsin.* In his 1846 title, *Wisconsin,* he makes an acute observation about the problem of habitat destruction:

> Several species of animals have already been compelled to leave Wisconsin by the approach of civilized men; and others are driven into the remote, unsettled portions, where they are probably destined to remain but a short time before they will, from the same cause, have to retire still further towards the "far west."

Lapham used his cartography skills to draw the first published map of the area in 1841. In all, he published about 80 titles, the most important of which were *Antiquities of Wisconsin,* which focused on Indian burial mounds including those at the prehistoric Aztalan site near present-day Lake Mills,

Increase A. Lapham
1811-1875

and *Report of the Disastrous Effects of the Destruction of Forest Trees,* a visionary conservation appeal. In the latter, he railed against the reckless deforestation of the pinery, warning that the result would be soil erosion and diminished stream flows.

Lapham's foresight was remarkable. He was among the first to advocate crop fertilization and rotation. He ensured that the 1843 territorial legislature adopted a resolution urging Congressional land grants for institutions for the blind, deaf, and insane. He was instrumental in establishing a federal weather service and served as Wisconsin's chief geologist from 1873 to 1875. Lapham's vast collection of natural history artifacts was acquired on behalf of the University of Wisconsin by the state legislature in 1876.

Wisconsin's first scholar and ecologist, Increase Lapham was a forerunner of such environment-minded citizens as John Muir, Aldo Leopold, Owen Gromme, and Gaylord Nelson.

Mt. Olive Lutheran Church (Milwaukee) confirmation class of 1909.

Chapter Two

BRAVE NEW WORLD

Wisconsin was for a time the boundary of the western frontier, and its rich soil, abundant wildlife, varied geologic formations, and vast stands of timber drew homesteaders of every race and religion. They came to escape the hardship, taxes, enforced military conscription, and religious persecution of their European homelands. They streamed to the Wisconsin wilderness from the squalor, noise, and confinement of large Eastern seaboard cities, and from poorer sections of the already-settled south.

The first big wave of immigrants to Wisconsin began in 1820, when southerners rode up the Mississippi River into the southwestern counties to take part in the lead mining boom. By 1836, the territorial census showed a total of 11,683 citizens. Four years later, that number had swollen nearly threefold to 30,945. By 1846, the territorial population was 155,277, and by the time of statehood in 1848 it exceeded 210,000.

Out of that number, about two-thirds were native-born Americans, and of those, all but about 6,800 had come from states north of Ohio and east of the Mississippi, according to statistics gathered in 1850. Most of these folks had immigrated from New York, a major port of entry into the country.

Of the one-third of the 1850 population that was foreign-born, most were from the British Isles. The Cornish miners who inhabited the Mineral Point area numbered about 7,000, but nearly half of them had left for California during the gold rush that began in 1849. Scots settled in Racine and

Betsy Thunder, probably of the Winnebago tribe, was a medicine woman who ministered to white settlers as well as her own people near Black River Falls in the late 1800s.

Courtesy Black River Falls Historical Society

Built in Dodgeville during the height of the lead mining boom, this 1835 log cabin is typical of those inhabited by settlers just arriving in Wisconsin. Notice the wooden shakes on the roof, cracked mud chinking between logs, and the absence of glass windows.

Rock counties, and the Welsh fanned out from Mineral Point to congregate in Dodgeville, and in Columbia and Waukesha counties. The Swiss settled New Glarus in Green County, and in Buffalo, Sauk and Taylor counties. The Dutch, Poles, Danes, and Baltic state immigrants settled here in lesser numbers.

Some came to establish new lives, leaving behind failed businesses, broken marriages, and debt. Ann Eliza Porter left Massachusetts in the late 1800s with her husband, hoping for better luck in the retail store business than they'd had in New England. On the way to Cooksville, Wisconsin, they came upon a man who brought his troubles along with him on his migration west. She describes her trepidation about this man's status as a murder suspect:

> Mr. Gross has been confined in the Madison jail since last October, the time of the murder, waiting his trial. He is about twenty-six years of age, and a pleasant, gentlemanly-looking man. I do not think he looks as though he could murder a man in cold blood and in broad daylight for the paltry sum of one hundred and fifty dollars. The result of his trial is doubtful, but I earnestly hope they do not convict him, and commit another murder.

Whatever their reasons for coming to Wisconsin, most settlers stayed, and with them their native customs, languages, and folklore, the threads of which still weave a strong warp and woof into the state's cultural fabric. These pioneers also brought with them the steadfast work ethic of their forebears and a dedication to progressive education, justice, and politics. But while retaining the cultural characteristics of their native countries, they were forging a collective identity as citizens of the United States of America.

Settling In

The prairie house was usually drafty. The wood used to build it had been cut while still green, and it would soon shrink so that the mud chinking between the logs came loose. The cold winter winds blew snow inside through the cracks, stealing much of the meager comfort offered by indoor fires. The roof was often constructed of wooden shakes, and the flooring was packed dirt or rough-hewn planks.

Furniture was crude, consisting of homemade stools and benches, tables fashioned from boards laid across pork or flour barrels, and beds of leaf-covered platforms or straw pallets. When they existed at all, windows were simply holes in the walls, for glass was much too expensive and difficult to transport.

Men had the challenging task of building the dwelling from whatever materials were at hand—materials ranging from limestone and fieldstone to wood and sod.

The men also undertook the rigorous job of breaking prairie sod for the first time. This involved using a "breaking plow" pulled by two oxen, which chewed through the thick root network of the turf. "Clearing bees" were common social gatherings, at which neighbors helped new farmers remove stumps and stones from fields.

In the rural north, many farmers had previously worked in the lumbering business. Some still did during the winter when their fields lay idle. Crime was almost non-existent. Most violence in rural areas was domestic in nature—arguments between fathers, sons, and brothers. Occasionally, individuals traveling along railways or on outlying roads were robbed, but such crimes were attributed to transients.

Most of the area's troubles took place in logging camps or the towns closest to them. In spring, the men returned from their long winter in the woods with money in their pockets and entertainment on their minds. When gangs of lumberjacks piled into the small northern towns, chaos could result.

Drinking establishments were prevalent. Many were equipped with brass foot rails, spittoons, woodstoves for heat, gas or kerosene light fixtures, and no chairs. "Bawdy houses," the polite term for brothels, housed permanent working residents, while others in the same profession operated out of seamy hotels or horse-drawn carriages. One particular such establishment in Tomahawk, still operating as a bed and breakfast, was built with secret tunnels in the cellar leading to a twin building across the street, affording quick and unnoticed getaways for patrons who wished to remain discreet during frequent police raids.

When the railroad arrived, it imported other diversions run by card sharps, "bunco artists," and their gambling entourages. These questionable characters were joined by "professional girls" who rode the rails from town to town with the sole mission of separating unsophisticated boys from their hard-earned cash. This infusion of new corruption brought with it increased crime.

Sidearms were legal in the latter half of the 19th century, and most men wore them at all times. Even women, particularly those who were single, concealed small, one-shot derringers in their purses to protect themselves from unwanted attention. As might be expected, the proliferation of

Frontier life had its diversions. These northern "Huck Finns" enjoy a universal summer pastime in a photo entitled "Fish'n In The Crick" by the photographer.

The locomotive shown was photographed in 1892 near Tomahawk, Wisconsin. Built in 1881 for the Minneapolis, Lyndale, and Minnetonka narrow-gauge street railway, the engine was purchased and converted to standard gauge in 1891 by the Soo Line Railway. It was leased in 1893 to the Wisconsin and Chippewa Railway, which purchased the locomotive outright in 1897 for $1,000. The engine eventually found its way to a logging company in Alabama and was scrapped in 1938, at the ripe old age of 57.

A farm family near Kavour, Wisconsin, poses for a portrait on their front porch. The milled lumber and real glass windows indicate that the house was probably built in the early 1900s. The bicycle in the foreground is a "velocipede," equipped with a third wheel designed to let the rider pedal on railroad tracks.

firearms led to a good deal of violence in the towns. As late as 1899, shoot-outs between lawmen and the criminals they were attempting to apprehend were not unheard of. Bank robbery and safecracking were two of the more common causes of such showdowns.

Normally, law enforcement in the towns, where populations were generally around 500, was carried out by a hired marshal or night watchman. This "police force" was supplemented with a single, temporary deputy during the spring and fall, when the lumberjacks shuttled to and from the camps. Because the towns had to choose their deputies from a limited number of available citizens, the character of those who enforced the law was sometimes as questionable as the character of those who might threaten the town.

One of the favorite pastimes of most men was hunting, an activity that was regulated poorly if at all near the turn of the century. Duck hunting, in particular, provided not only sport and recreation, but a good livelihood. Full-time duck hunters along the lower Wolf River were headquartered in floating shanties, the earliest of which were often shelters called "wanigans" that had been discarded by lumber operations. Cannon-like "punt" guns were used, and these boomers could bag a hundred birds with a single shot. The hapless fowl were drawn into range with the aid of live decoys, which were also legal at the time. The birds were sold to fancy restaurants in large cities like New York.

A Woman's Work

Rural settlement had its dangers, but Lucinda Holton, wife of prominent Milwaukee politician Edward Holton, wrote about one of the worries that plagued even a resident of a "civilized" town in 1850:

Had a great fright tonight from fire. The wind is blowing a perfect hurricane outside, the most terrific I ever knew. I had a good fire built in my room, babies both asleep, and was just settling myself for a pleasant evening when we discovered our chimney on fire. Edward out of town and no man about the house. Maria [the hired girl] was almost frantic. No damage done, however . . . By throwing on salt, it was soon extinguished.

A feeling of isolation from other human beings was common among the pioneers, particularly women like Lucinda, whose husbands were often absent from the homestead. Some men worked in distant towns for wages to help get their new farms going; some rode off to get supplies; others died during or soon after the settlement journey, from various ailments. A frontier wife often had to run the new farm by herself, sometimes with no previous experience.

In addition to cleaning and caring for children, a homestead wife tended livestock such as cows, goats, pigs, and sheep. The animals were often evil-tempered creatures, much less domesticated than the ones we raise today. The wife chopped and hauled wood. If she was lucky, she drew water from a well; if she wasn't, she toted it from a river or stream.

Other tasks, such as washing clothes and linens, could take an entire day when one had to haul the necessary water, boil it, make soap from ashes and lard, scrub the clothes on a washboard, and hang them out to dry. A pioneer woman made her own candles, rendered her own lamp oil, churned butter if she was fortunate enough to have a lactating cow or goat, and carded and spun wool so she could knit warm winter garments.

Most families did without any doctoring other than what they could manage themselves, with Mother

These rural Glandon women, probably a mother and her daughters, share the joys of baking from scratch in a wood-fired stove.

A center for social events as well as worship, this modest wooden church was built amidst the debris of a timber cutover.

usually assuming the role of physician. According to a cherished legend from Wisconsin's history, the paths from a pioneer woman's door led in all directions, indicating her willingness to care not only for her own family, but for any friends and neighbors who needed her.

Tough Medicine

No house was without its store of "home remedies" in the cupboard. Any number of teas, ointments, liniments and herbal cures shared the shelves with potions, vile-smelling oils, and extracts bought from traveling medicine shows. One Columbus woman wrote of her childhood fascination with such a show:

> Each summer, "The Medicine Show" came to Columbus. The railroad car in which the company lived was switched to a siding just off Birdsey Street, the big tent was pitched, and for six nights the show was on. It consisted of vaudeville acts which were interspersed with hawkers running up and down the aisles shouting their wares. In this case it was bottles of the "Elixir of Youth."
>
> Father always bought a bottle, and our mother said it was for this that father took us to see the show at least twice a week.

Among the more common home remedies were:

- butter, sugar, and ginger, mixed together to soothe children's coughs;

- goose grease and mustard, rubbed on chest for colds or backaches;

- flax seed, cooked for use as a laxative or ground for poultices;

- May apple for liver ailments and constipation;

- touch-me-not blossoms rubbed on the skin to soothe irritations.

Indigestion was treated with rhubarb bitters or cayenne pepper poultices applied to the abdomen. Pleurisy called for a chest poultice, which could be made of boiled hot nettles or catnip with pennyroyal or butterfly weed tea. Mixtures of pokeberries in brandy or calomel, cayenne pepper and gum camphor were prescribed for arthritis flare-ups.

Travelling "medicine men" perfected the art of door-to-door salesmanship long before the Fuller brush man became a regular phenomenon. Rose Schuster Taylor was a child on a Middleton farm just before the Civil War, and remembered:

This bottle contained a curative designed to heal the afflictions of several organs.

I believe I hated the worm tablets that he sold the most of all. They were huge, pink wafers that were bitter to my tongue. To this day, I can still wake up at night and shudder at the thought of those pink wafers.

In particularly vexing cases, midwives, spirit healers, and other traditionalists were called in to treat the ailing patient. For acute attacks like appendicitis, someone was sent to fetch the nearest doctor, but he often arrived too late to save the sick person. Surgical operations were sometimes performed in the less-than-sterile environment of the kitchen table.

Childbirth was a leading cause of death among women and their babies. The first recorded quintuplets were born in February of 1875 in Watertown to Edward and Edna Karouse. Because even one-child births were difficult and dangerous without sterile conditions, the five babies didn't stand much of a chance. All died within two weeks of their entry into the world.

Pioneer children who survived spent much of their time working on family farms, and often went to school only through the eighth grade, if they got that far. Help was scarce, and all available bodies were needed to keep the farms running all year long. Even after public schools were established and machinery was introduced to help farmers with their work, children often took a year or two off between elementary school and high school.

This solitary, difficult life took its toll on many of the early settlers of Wisconsin. Some returned to their homes in the East or across the sea. Some became victims of smallpox, cholera, scarlet fever, or the other diseases that were unchecked by vaccinations or regular medical treatment. Still others succumbed to the rigors of a life that demanded more than they had to give. Those who remained, however, put down deep roots and established a network of farms and industries that eventually provided the ingredients for "America's Breadbasket."

In late autumn, or early winter, the medicine man was sure to appear. For every ailment he had a panacea. There was rheumatism enough to go around, and liniment sales were big. We bought it by the quart. It was to be rubbed in frequently, regularly, and abundantly.

His sweet balsam syrup tasted so pleasant, she added, that the children would cough whether they were sick or not, just to get some.

Another Sand County woman, this one from Montello, wonders:

How I ever survived my childhood has always been a mystery to me. I firmly believe that no child on the face of this earth ever went through the curative treatments that my mother inflicted on me and my brothers and sisters. How I used to dread the arrival of the Watkins man! When he used to rattle up into our farmyard in his old Model T Ford, I knew instinctively that I was in for it again.

When the Kashube people fled their native Poland and the persecution of Kaiser Wilhelm's Prussian dictatorship in the 1870s, many of them settled on Milwaukee's tiny Jones Island. A fishing boat and two dories are moored behind their crowded homes.

A Colorful Weave

One of the most remarkable aspects of Wisconsin's settlement is the fact that a broad spectrum of ethnic groups located here. To this day, Milwaukee is a microcosm of this diversity. Although the city's earliest residents were of French and English descent, its first black citizen, Joe Oliver, worked as a cook for influential architect Solomon Juneau and in 1835 voted in the town's first election.

In 1848, after German farmers had experienced major crop failures for the previous two years, many emigrated to America. Not finding the "good life" they had sought in their first location (mostly near the steel mills of Pittsburgh, Pennsylvania), they headed for the Midwest. The federal government encouraged this settlement by offering land for a little over a dollar an acre.

By 1880, so many Germans lived in Milwaukee that English was a minority language. German was taught in both public and parochial schools from the first grade forward. Parents were required to get permission to exempt children from such classes. German was so widely accepted that a person who wanted to shop on North Third Street needed to speak it in order to complete transactions in that Old World section of town.

Milwaukee also became home to the Kashubes, laborers and fishermen who had immigrated from West Prussia in 1870. Regarded as lower-class citizens by the Poles who preceded them, the Kashubes settled on tiny Jones Island at the mouth of the Milwaukee River. Expert fishermen and net-knitters, they were a rowdy, independent lot who spoke their own dialect and had no written language.

The island's men had a reputation for being willing and capable fighters, always ready for a brawl. This combativeness came in handy many times as

These fair maids sport traditional Dutch garb at the German Bazaar in 1916, a precursor to Milwaukee's annual Holiday Folk Fair celebration.

they fended off rivals who came to steal their island girls, thought by mainland boys to be great beauties. Island children were rowed across the water to school at St. Stanislaus in warm weather, and walked across the ice in winter. At its peak, Jones Island boasted 2,200 residents, seven stores, and 11 saloons.

Felix Struck was the first Kashube born on Jones Island. At 13, he had run off to sea, and at 14 found himself stranded in South Chicago, penniless. Interviewed for a book about Jones Island, he recalled:

> I walked into a saloon. A real friendly sailor offered me a drink. Of course, I was only too glad to accept his offer. That drink was the last thing I remembered. Hours later I was aboard the schooner Collins, far out in the lake on the way to Buffalo. She carried a load of pig-iron. Of course I knew I had been kidnapped; but since I couldn't get off, I made the best of it.

That was how Struck became acquainted with whiskey, which provided his livelihood for many years. In the winter of 1944 Struck, then 73, closed the Harbor Saloon, where he had quenched the thirst of thousands of Great Lakes sailors for 45 years.

By 1920 only 25 Kashube families remained. The city paid them for condemnation rights so a sewage treatment plant could be built on the site, and the families gradually died out or straggled away to other locales. When Felix Struck shut down his saloon, it signaled the end of an era in Milwaukee's immigrant history.

The Kashubes also settled in Two Rivers, Manitowoc, and Port Washington from 1850 to the 1870s. At about the same time, Poles emigrated to Wisconsin after the invasion of their homeland by Bismarck's Prussian army, settling in Cassel and Reitbrock. After the formation of the Austro-Hungarian Empire in 1867, Norwegians and Bohemians also appeared. The Norwegians settled mainly in Elderon. Other Scandinavian immigrants, along with many Bohemians, ended up near Mosinee and Racine.

The Wisconsin Valley Railroad was selling off much of its right-of-way acreage in order to promote settlement and the use of rail services. The company went so far as to send agents to recruit settlers from Germany and from German-speaking Switzerland. By century's end, 70 percent of Marathon County's foreign-born settlers were German.

John Fogg's saloon on Jones Island hosted the "Cannibal's Rendezvous," a ritual of unknown significance, in the 1880s. Fogg's business was one of 11 taverns on the tiny island at the mouth of the Milwaukee River.

Here Come the Gypsies

Gypsies had traveled from India in the mid-14th century, peculiar in their nomadic lifestyle. Their habit of wandering from town to town, with no apparent roots, aroused suspicion among the close-knit and parochial citizens of Europe. Many of the Gypsies, feeling unwelcome in their adopted homeland, struck out for America with the rest of Europe's emigrants in the great rush before the turn of the century.

They came to Wisconsin in their colorful wagons, and were commonly seen by the early 1900s. Characterized by their flamboyant manners, flashy jewelry, and mismatched clothing, they camped in caravans outside of towns and villages, visiting residents to beg or offering to read palms for money. Although it was rumored that the Gypsies were prone to stealing vegetables from unwatched gardens, or might even snatch a pie cooling on a windowsill, most country folks seemed genuinely fond of them. Some farmers allowed Gypsies to camp on their land and exchanged gifts with them.

Charlotte Hawley gives us a picture of this wary alliance in her essay, "Remembering The Gypsies." They traveled through her southern Wisconsin farm area every summer, their arrival heralded by the clopping of horses' hooves on a wooden overpass east of the farm. She recalls their visits just after the turn of the century:

> For years, Gypsies had stayed in the far corner of our pasture. It was an isolated spot that offered utmost privacy and provided water for the animals. Except for an occasional visit from one or two members of the caravan, the Gypsies never disturbed us. This astonished our neighbors, who complained of a variety of felonies and misdemeanors. Perhaps the Gypsies wanted to safeguard their short-term campground.
>
> At any event, they'd loot our neighbor's hen house, but tell Mama's fortune for a thank-you. They'd steal another neighbor's jewelry, but leave good luck amulets for [my cousin] Maggie and me. Once they sold a horse to the sheriff's deputy. It was dyed, drugged with herbs, and through remarkable trickery made to appear as

spry as a mountain goat. The Gypsies were miles away by the time the prancing steed turned into a limping old clod. Yet another time, they treated our lame horse with an herbal potion and had him back in the fields within a week.

In his book *The Land Remembers*, Ben Logan tells of his first encounter with Gypsies. He describes the wagon that pulled up in front of the family's farm in Gays Mills, Wisconsin:

> The driver was a woman, sitting on a little seat that was protected by a curving roof. She wore a long purple skirt, a purple scarf on her head, and a white blouse with ribbons and lace.
>
> "Come quick. It's Gypsies!" Mother called.
>
> Only Lee and I were close. We were already watching from back by the woodshed. All our lives we'd heard tales of how the Gypsies stole children. Mother was waiting beside the porch with a big loaf of bread. They smiled at her, gave their funny little bow, and ran to the wagon, gold earrings and bracelets dancing.
>
> Mother called, "Get some apples. And a few eggs." We ran to the orchard and picked up the fallen apples. I went on to the chicken house and took six eggs from the nests. We ran back to the wagon and handed the eggs and apples up to the woman. She nodded with each handful. The big smile flashed again. She reached out, touched both of us lightly on top of the head, and said something we couldn't understand.

It seems that the amount of respect the Gypsies showed for their hosts was in direct proportion to the degree of kindness extended. Gypsies appeared well into the middle of the 20th century, adapting to auto travel in the late 1920s.

In God We Trust

When immigrants first came to Wisconsin, often the only reminder of home they were able to bring with them was their religious faith. Investing time, energy, and wealth in their churches brought settlers the comfort of continuity, and the feeling of having some control over life in their new land.

This in turn created a widespread commitment to religious life that has endured throughout the state's history.

In settlement days, isolated areas were served by circuit-riding preachers. They prayed, provided sacraments for baptisms, marriages, and funerals and—most importantly—brought contact with the outside world. But as the state grew in size and cultural sophistication, churches were built or services were held in the basements of school buildings, and some unique religious practices emerged.

"King" Strang

James Jesse Strang, a young zealot, had written in his diary at age 19: "All I know is that I am eager and mankind are frail. I shall act upon [this knowledge] in times to come for my own benefit." Strang embraced the concept of free-thinking rationalism advanced in Thomas Paine's book, The Age of Reason, and was cast out of his Baptist church for his heretical ideas. He left his hometown of Chautauqua, New York, took a bride, and moved to Burlington, Wisconsin.

In Burlington, Strang met many Mormon converts, and so he traveled in 1844 to Nauvoo, Illinois, in order to learn about the faith from founder Joseph Smith. Baptized and made an elder, Strang left Nauvoo to search for a new Mormon site in Wisconsin. Upon hearing of Smith's assassination a month later, Strang proclaimed his divine ordination as the new prophet of the Mormons. He was promptly denounced by other elders and voted out of the church.

Undaunted, Strang left for Burlington and recruited "saints" for his paradise, which he christened Voree. He claimed that the name meant "Garden of Peace," and he had grandiose plans for his communistic settlement of 2,000, including marble architecture and a community university. He stimulated recruitment by borrowing a trick from Joseph Smith, who had initiated Mormonism by digging golden plates from a hillside 18 years earlier.

Strang led four disciples to an oak tree on what he

Charismatic religious leader James Jesse Strang as he appeared about a year before he was killed by two of his own followers in 1856.

had dubbed the "Hill of Promise," where they "discovered" three copper plates engraved with mysterious symbols. Strang was able to "translate" the message, which prophesied his own divine selection. The revelation spread through the country, drawing pilgrims to Voree.

Soon new converts were flocking to the booming settlement. But too many saints in one place soon turned the Garden of Peace into something other than paradise. In 1847, with squabbles rife among the residents of Voree, Strang announced that a new colony would be built on Beaver Island in Lake Michigan. However, nearby settlers proved hostile to the newcomers.

The Strang cottage at Voree, the settlement established for breakaway Mormons near Burlington, Wisconsin. Strang told his followers that Voree meant "Garden of Peace."

On July 3, 1850, some neighboring fishermen moored their boats near Beaver Island to have a few shots of whiskey before attacking the new commune. But rumors of the attack had reached Strang, and his followers discouraged the fishermen with cannon fire, effectively aborting the siege.

Four days later, Strang had himself crowned King in a lavish coronation ceremony, and his subjects took an oath of loyalty to him. He authorized polygamy, because he had become enamored of his secretary, a woman named Elvira Field, and wanted her to legally share his bed. Because he was already married, he saw authorized polygamy as the only answer, despite the fact that he had previously denounced the practice.

The following May, President Millard Fillmore sent armed guards to detain Strang and three of his apostles on charges of treason, robbing the mails, and counterfeiting. Having practiced law in New York in his younger days, Strang defended himself as a religious martyr and was acquitted. Amazingly, he was later elected twice to the Michigan legislature and gained three other wives.

In 1856, Strang met his demise at the hands of two disgruntled former "saints" who ambushed and fatally shot him.

Holy Hill

Possibly the most celebrated religious shrine in Wisconsin, Holy Hill has a long and intriguing history. According to legend, Pere (Father) Marquette erected the first cross on this hill in the northern Kettle Moraine during a visit in 1673. Immigrants later cleared the surrounding land for farms, and a German priest, one Father Paulhuber, bought the hill from the U.S. government for $50 in 1855, envisioning pilgrimages from throughout the nation.

Nine years later, a hermit was discovered kneeling at the base of the 15-foot oak cross that had recently been planted at the top of the hill. The hermit was Francois Soubrio, who was then living in a cave on the hill's eastern side.

While studying for the priesthood as a young man in Strasbourg, France, Soubrio had fallen in love with a young woman, and had renounced his vows of celibacy. He later discovered that his fiancee was in love with someone else and murdered her in a jealous rage.

Fleeing to Quebec, Ontario, Soubrio became a recluse in an old monastery there and came across one of Pere Marquette's diaries, in which the famous black robe recounted his travels to Holy

This drawing depicts the first small chapel built on Holy Hill in 1865. The humble cabin was a far cry from the imposing red brick monastery with twin towers that now graces the Kettle Moraine landmark.

Hill, which he had dedicated as holy ground. Soubrio felt compelled to see this place for himself and immediately set out for America. Coming ashore in Chicago, he began making his way north to the land Marquette described in the diary.

Soubrio fell ill on this journey and became partially paralyzed. After many trials, he finally struggled to the top of the hill, where he collapsed. When he awoke, he found that his paralysis had vanished. Word of Holy Hill's healing power soon spread far and wide.

The year after Soubrio was discovered at the base of the cross, a log chapel was erected. The shrine was first referred to as "Holy Hill" in a sermon delivered there. A brick church replaced the log chapel in 1881. Milwaukee's archdiocese urged the Carmelite order of friars to administer the church, and the first of these friars arrived in 1906. The current monastery atop Holy Hill attracts thousands of the faithful and the curious every year, and it ranks as one of the state's most popular visitor destinations.

Family Traditions

Nowhere is the ethnic influence on Wisconsin culture so apparent as in holiday celebrations and food preparation. Historian Art Lee wrote about post-World War II life in his aptly named home-town of Scandinavia, near Waupaca. In his book, The Lutefisk Ghetto, he shares memories of the sumptuous Christmas Eve feast enjoyed by his family:

> Much preparation was necessary for this night, notably the baking of Fattigman, Berliner, Sandbakkels and Krumkake. Big loaves of Julebrod were in the pantry, flanked by piles of lefse and flatbrod, and the barrel of apples was opened.

Mrs. Elizabeth Opdahl and her daughters Karen, Leonharda, and Anna were members of a prominent Norwegian immigrant family in Wausau. They operated the "Skandinavia House" hotel, which catered especially to lumberjacks of Scandinavian descent. Here, they pose for a Christmas portrait in 1900.

Mrs. Fritz Bauer, granddaughter of a German who emigrated to Milwaukee to open the city's first toy store, recalls a family Christmas in which their "bunte Teller," an old-time soup plate with a broad, flat rim, was filled with:

> A large California orange in the center, almonds, hazelnuts, walnuts and Brazil nuts in the shell, surrounding the orange. Arranged neatly over this were hazelnut Lebkuchen, honey Lebkuchen, Pfaster steine, weisse-und-braune Pfeffernuesse, natural yellow butter cookies, old fashioned chocolate drops, miniature fruits and vegetables [made] of marzipan. Add to this glistening colored French creams and a white or brown mouse [made] of French cream with pink frosting eyes and a snout and tail of brown twine.

Mrs. Bauer apologizes for relating the names of the items in German, but insists that, "When translated into English, the charm is lost."

The Swiss in New Glarus rang out the old year with church bells and the tooting of whistles at the milk condensary, the brewery, and the train depot. Tables loaded with heavy pear bread, crumbly coffee cake, cookies, and homemade wines awaited gatherings of families and friends. Fresh cream, whipped stiff with hazelnut switches, was served from a huge common bowl at the center of the table. Some revelers lobbed spoonfuls of the cream at each other until they were covered with it, resembling the snowmen outside.

BADGER PROFILE: The Working Woman's Friend

Christopher Sholes learned the printer's trade in Danville, Pennsylvania, and moved to Wisconsin in 1837. He joined his brothers Henry and Charles, who had settled in Green Bay. Together, they published a local newspaper called the *Wisconsin Democrat.* Two years later, he moved to Madison to manage the staff of the *Wisconsin Enquirer,* and in 1840 Sholes established the *Southport Telegraph* in what is now Kenosha. He published this newspaper for 17 years with a variety of partners, including pioneer education reformer Michael Frank. After 1857, he had brief associations with several Milwaukee newspapers, including the *Wisconsin Free Democrat*, the *News,* and the *Sentinel.*

Sholes, an avid abolitionist, was originally a Democrat supporting Andrew Jackson, but he later helped organize the Free Soil and Republican parties. He moved on to the Liberal Republicans and finally to the Greenback party. He served for two terms as state senator and one as state assemblyman. During the Civil War, Sholes also acted as Milwaukee's postmaster, port collector, and commissioner of public works.

Sholes is perhaps best-known, however, as an inventor. His patented innovations include a printer's paging and numbering device invented in 1864 and a newspaper addressing machine. His frustration with the inefficiency of handwritten articles led him to alliances with various partners in the pursuit of a machine that would produce mechanical lettering, and in 1867 he produced his first crude prototype. By 1869, he had perfected the first functional "typewriter" while working at C.F. Kleinstuber's machine shop in Milwaukee.

After gaining some financial backing and promotional help, Sholes developed 40 more sophisticated models before coming up with one in 1872 that would be the basis of all future standard typewriters. It lacked a carriage shift and a front keystroke as we know them today, but Sholes continued to work at his invention. Unable to make any basic improvements, he sold his interest

Courtesy State Historical Society of Wisconsin

Christopher Latham Sholes
1804-1894

in the machine to his original financial backer, James Densmore, for $12,000 in 1872. Densmore contracted the following year with E. Remington & Sons, whose firearms factories had the kind of precise tooling needed to produce the writing machine in quantity.

The first commercially available machine was dubbed "The Sholes and Glidden Typewriter." One of these was used to produce Mark Twain's *Tom Sawyer,* believed to be the first typed manuscript ever submitted to a printer.

Asked if he thought his invention had done "a wonderful thing for the world," Sholes replied, "I don't know about the world, but I do feel that I have done something for the women who have always had to work so hard. It will enable them more easily to earn a living." He died before the first typewriter was introduced to the state capitol in Madison, but within 50 years more than 2,000 of the machines were in active state service, and over 90 percent of them were operated by women.

BADGER PROFILE: Angel On Snowshoes

Dr. Kate Pelham Newcomb
1885-1956

Kate Pelham was born in Leoti, Kansas in 1885, to Kate Callahan Pelham, a schoolteacher, and Thomas Pelham, an ambitious schoolteacher-turned-banker. When Kate was just a few years old, her mother died in childbirth, leaving her small daughter devastated. Soon after, Thomas ended his mourning period by marrying his late wife's best friend, Nona Fenton, who was also young Kate's godmother.

The family moved to Abilene, Kansas and then to Buffalo, New York, in pursuit of better employment prospects. Kate clung to her mother's memory, and when she graduated from grade school in 1900, she decided to honor that memory by following her mother into the teaching profession. Although it wasn't a vocation that especially suited Kate's desires or temperament, it was one of the few careers available to the young women of her day.

Remembering her mother's untimely death in the throes of childbirth, Kate really wanted to pursue a career in obstetrics, hoping to prevent other small children from being left motherless in such a sad and brutal way. But her father wouldn't hear of it, declaring that medicine was "no profession for a lady." Since he was paying for her education, she was compelled to settle for teaching. Kate finished high school and completed the required year of teacher's training, then began teaching sixth and seventh grades in the Buffalo public school system.

Thomas Pelham's new position as Gillette Razor Company's corporate counsel then required him to move his family to Boston, Massachusetts. Kate remained in Buffalo, rooming with fellow teacher Mabel Walters. Mabel introduced Kate to the Women's Christian Temperance Union, whose great variety of activities intrigued Kate and took her mind off past sorrows and the absence of her siblings. Through her new friends, she met a sympathetic woman doctor who encouraged her not to give up her dream of practicing medicine.

By this time, Thomas had become president of Gillette. When Nona died suddenly, he summoned Kate to Boston to help him care for the children and assume hostess duties at his social gatherings. This didn't appeal to Kate, but Thomas was adamant, so she reluctantly packed her things. She was miserable in her society role, and made no secret of it.

Eventually, after Kate had committed a number of social gaffes, her father admitted that she wasn't cut out for the role of hostess. He allowed her to begin the study of medicine at his expense. Kate returned to Buffalo and began her studies in September of 1913. She was 28 years old.

After four difficult years, she graduated cum laude from the University of Buffalo, and proceeded to look for an internship. She found one in Detroit, Michigan, at the Women's Hospital, but it wasn't available until that fall, so she took a temporary visiting nurse position in the slums of New York's "Little Italy."

It was a baptism by fire into the realm of real-world obstetrics for the woman who came to be known as "Lady Doc." Her endless hours, the abject poverty of her patients, and the unsanitary conditions of the poorly ventilated, squalid tenements gave Kate a genuine appreciation of the clean, modern Women's Hospital in Detroit when she finally arrived there.

She served her internship during the war years of 1917 to 1919 under three female obstetricians. When she began private practice, her father presented her with a new automobile. At that time, cars came with driving lessons. Kate fell in love with and married her instructor, Bill Newcomb, a native of Michigan.

Kate next accepted a staff position at the hospital, where she was asked to become an assistant to her medical school mentor in his research on childhood diseases. Dr. David Levy was one of the finest pediatricians in the country, and this association put Kate Pelham Newcomb, M.D., at the top of her profession. Everything had fallen into place for Dr. Kate.

But paradise on earth is a short-lived proposition, and misfortune appeared on the horizon with a marked deterioration in Bill's health. He became pale, weak, and lethargic, refusing food and eventually giving up his job. A battery of tests determined that Bill was suffering the after-effects of his wartime work in a metals plant, where he had inhaled toxic fumes from acids used to treat the metal. The poisoning had resulted in acute anemia, and unless he could move from the city to a place offering clean, fresh air, his condition could be fatal.

Bill went to stay with his parents just outside of Milwaukee. He made plans to travel to northern Wisconsin, where the air agreed with him and his health improved considerably. Kate found herself miserable without Bill so, ten months after her big promotion, she left the hospital and joined him at his parents' home. They boarded a lumber train for the northwoods and debarked in Eagle River, then just a lumber camp station. It was New Year's Day, 1922.

The couple moved into a crude cabin 18 miles away and settled into rural life. Kate nursed Bill back to health, and soon they discovered that an addition to the family was on the way. They moved to Stone Lake, where they rented a cottage with more "modern" conveniences, such as an acetylene stove and gas lanterns. Kate maintained a correspondence with Dr. Levy, who kept her up-to-date on the latest medical developments, and she found a doctor in nearby Crandon to attend to her delivery.

Tragically, the baby lived for only 48 hours, victim of a new delivery method called "twilight sleep," in which heavy sedatives are used to dull labor pains. The practice was later condemned by the medical profession. Wild with grief and embittered toward medicine, Kate renounced her profession. She and Bill moved to an abandoned logging camp and became ordinary northwoods residents. After a forest fire nearly burned down their home, they moved again to Rice Creek near Boulder Junction in 1926, where Bill became a hunting and fishing guide. They soon had another child, and this one survived.

In 1931, Kate received a call from Dr. T.G. Torpy, the only practicing physician in the area, who was treating patients as far north as the Wisconsin-Michigan border. He had been informed that she was a retired doctor, and wanted her to make a call on a patient who lived near her. An unrefined man with a tendency to be brusque, he bullied her into making the call. She strapped on snowshoes to reach the homebound patient, ending her ten-year hiatus from medicine.

She eventually took over the northern half of Dr. Torpy's territory, operating out of her Boulder Junction home. Gas rationing in the war years required her to be closer to her patients, so in 1942 she opened an office in Woodruff. It included a tiny living area in the back, where she stayed when bad weather prevented her from returning to

Boulder Junction. Though the weather may have kept her from home, it never kept her from her rounds. When all other means of transportation failed, she was not above strapping on her snowshoes and trudging through the drifts and driving snow to care for ailing patients, earning her an affectionate sobriquet, "Angel On Snowshoes."

In a unique pediatrics practice, she delivered over 4,000 babies—in their homes, since there was no hospital—treated them for childhood ailments, and tended also to the health of their mothers. Although she missed the camaraderie of working with other doctors, Dr. Kate found country doctoring to her liking. "You know your patients," she commented, "their family backgrounds and their problems."

She saw between 20 and 45 patients and averaged 100 miles per day on her car. She was very disturbed that the patients had to travel long distances to Rhinelander or Tomahawk for care beyond what she could provide. She founded the Lakeland Memorial Hospital, built with funds from a penny drive initiated by local students. The "Million Penny Parade" gained national recognition and catapulted the backwoods physician to fame when she appeared in 1954 on Ralph Edwards' television program, *This Is Your Life*.

The Lakeland area was shocked and deeply saddened when Dr. Kate succumbed in 1956 to complications of surgery on a broken hip and died at the age of 70.

The Dr. Kate Museum is now housed on the lot where her Woodruff clinic stood, a fitting tribute to a woman whose courage and kindness allowed her to overcome personal tragedy and contribute to the welfare of those around her. The life of the "Angel On Snowshoes" proves that community is a state of mind and a matter of heart, not a geographical site.

Chapter Three

IN PURSUIT OF TRUTH

The inquiry of truth, which is the lovemaking, or wooing of it; the knowledge of truth, which is the presence of it; and the belief of truth, which is the enjoying of it; is the sovereign good of human nature.

—*Sir Francis Bacon*

Two of the most telling characteristics of any society are the laws it makes to govern itself and the way in which it educates its young people. In both respects, Wisconsin has revealed itself as a liberal and progressive state.

Just after statehood, the 1850 census showed that Wisconsin was home to 305,000 people. That number more than doubled, increasing to 775,000, by the time the 1860 census was tabulated. In both censuses, over a third of the people were foreign-born citizens, and by 1860 over half of that fraction were German immigrants. The German-born citizens tended to congregate in Milwaukee, Manitowoc, and Washington counties and, due to their generally superior education, wielded social and political influence out of proportion to their numbers.

The great wave of German emigration to the United States in 1848 was partly a result of the homeland's conservative government and its determined attempt to quash liberal thought in Germany. Many of the talented intellectuals who moved from Germany to the U.S. held unorthodox

This building housed the Ripon Congregational Church and served as a meeting place for the founders of a new political party in 1854. It has since been known as the "Birthplace of the Republican Party."

Wausau's first high school teacher, W.A. Gordon (far right), poses with the graduating class of 1857. Gordon looks sufficiently stern as his erstwhile students hold an open book and an abacus to underscore their earnest pursuit of knowledge.

political and religious beliefs. They fled to the purported freedom of America to build tightly knit communities whose ambitions mirrored those of their founders. One of the foremost goals of these immigrants was to establish a system of high-quality education that encouraged critical analysis and free thought.

A Land to Call Our Own

In 1855 the Democrats still held power in Wisconsin, as they had since the proclamation of statehood. The previous year, various members of the Whig, Free Democrat, Free Soil, and Know Nothing parties had become enraged over what was called the "Nebraska Swindle," an arrangement under which Nebraska and Kansas territories had been admitted to the nation by the Democratic administration. The uproar was caused by the choice given the newcomers of allowing slavery or declaring it illegal. That such a choice should even be considered, much less legislated, outraged many northerners, who considered slavery the greatest moral evil of their time.

Alan Bovay, a prominent Whig, assembled these sundry party members at the Old Congregational Church in Ripon in February of 1854, bent on forming a new political party. The new party's purpose was to protest the slavery issue, and the name "Republican" was suggested by Bovay.

That March, following the new party's Ripon assembly, an event took place that would galvanize the already surging abolitionist sentiment. Joshua Glover, an escaped black slave, was working in a Racine mill. His owner, B.S. Garland, traveled to Milwaukee and applied for a warrant to capture and return Glover to Missouri. Federal marshals accompanied Garland to a Racine cabin, where Glover was arrested, beaten, and taken to the Milwaukee County Jail.

Sherman Booth, feisty editor of the *Milwaukee Free Democrat,* rode through Milwaukee streets shouting "Freemen! To the rescue!" He aroused the passions of a mob that stormed the jail and smuggled Glover to freedom in Canada. For his actions, Booth was arrested under the Fugitive Slave Act, and his case quickly became the talk of the day. For six years, Booth was in and out of jail as the result of ensuing court battles. He was finally pardoned by President Buchanan in the last days of his presidency before Lincoln took over in 1861.

The Glover Incident, as it came to be known, lent immediacy to the fledgling movement. Bovay's suggested name for the new party was sent to the *New York Tribune* in a letter to publisher Horace Greeley. Greeley was a strong antislavery advocate, and his weekly newspaper was a powerful molder of public opinion throughout the North.

Inside Babcock's primary school, students sit for a portrait in the grammar room. A large, ornate woodstove provides heat for the room. The stove was also useful for drying wet mittens and warming soup for lunch.

A resolution to officially adopt the "Republican" name was cheered by 3,000 delegates at the first Wisconsin convention in July. One facet of this resolution was the invitation to "all persons, whether of native or foreign birth" to join the party—an act of good faith notably absent from the charters of previously established political parties. It was a strategic move on the part of the Republicans to gain the much-courted support of the state's foreign-born majority.

An up-and-coming young politico, Carl Schurz (see profile), saw the tide rising in favor of the abolitionist movement, and prophesied events soon to come in an 1857 letter to a friend:

> At last the slavery issue has become the issue of the day; the time for compromise has passed, and the last chance for a peaceful solution has come. The next few years will decide the fate of the United States. I do not know whether this struggle can be decided without powder, I hardly think so. However, should the force of arms be resorted to . . . the result cannot be doubtful, for the material superiority of the North is immense.

The Republican Party nominated its first candidate in the presidential election of 1860, and Schurz helped stump for Abraham Lincoln, the man who eventually forged the Emancipation Proclamation. Schurz was credited with much of Lincoln's campaign success.

A Passion for Learning

Wisconsin's history as a bastion of liberal education pre-dates its state charter. The Northwest Ordinance of 1787 required the surveying of townships six miles square, with one square mile set aside for the use of schools. Although this ordinance was forward-looking, it was also somewhat

Such ornate and well-built schools as this Augusta High School building (1909) testified to the importance placed on education, especially considering that many of the students' families at the time lived in small, wood-frame houses.

An eighth-grade class photo taken at a West Side Milwaukee school in about 1909.

shortsighted, in that it provided no money for the development of school lands.

It did, however, create the framework for the educational portion of the Territorial Land Act of 1846, which designated the set-aside land as Section 16 of each surveyed township, to be leased by school commissioners appointed by each town. Each taxable property within each township was to be assessed a school tax to pay for the construction and maintenance of buildings and for teachers' salaries. These sections of land were to be reserved from government land sales and granted to Wisconsin upon its attainment of statehood.

Congress also granted Wisconsin, upon statehood, 500,000 additional acres for unspecified internal improvements. The state constitution allotted these for school use. Certain other public land proceeds, fines, forfeitures, and unassigned state grants were also delegated to the "school fund." Federal lands

granted for university support were added, and their proceeds were earmarked for perpetual educational funds.

These lands consisted of two townships, or 46,080 acres, and any taxes or other levies collected from them were forever to be allotted for education. The state constitutional charter also required the legislature to provide by law for district schools "free and without charge for tuition to all children between the ages of four and twenty years; and no sectarian instruction shall be allowed therein," a uniquely progressive approach for its time.

The Way It Was

Prior to statehood, Wisconsin provided what schooling it could for its young people. Without taxation to pay for schools, only parents who could afford books, part of the teacher's salary, and a "wood tax" (in payment for wood burned in the school's stove) could send their children to school. Education was thus a luxury available only to the relatively well-off, not a universal entitlement.

Before communities could afford to build separate school buildings, classes were often held in the basements of churches or other public buildings. When a school building was available, it was most likely a one-room affair housing grades one through six or one through eight, and taught by a single teacher. The furniture consisted of rough benches for pupils and a simple table and chair for the schoolmaster. Law required that schools in rural areas could not be built more than two miles apart, to ensure reasonable walking distances for pupils.

The teacher was usually female, with an average of one or two years of normal school (teacher's training). She might be as young as 16, and she would generally board with a nearby farm family. Like her pupils, she carried a pail lunch to school. The boarding family would offer this service in lieu of paying the salary fee. Earlier, the teacher would board with each pupil's family for a week at a time, to spread out the cost among the families.

One of the few male teachers was Daniel Thomas, who sailed in 1851 from Buffalo, New York. Arriving in Milwaukee, he hitched a ride on a haywagon to the small town of Kingston. He worked among farmers there for room and board—milking, haying, and doing general errands for two years. Finding the work tedious and the pay unacceptable, Thomas took a teaching exam in 1853 and began teaching in Kingston township.

After he got used to the profession, he transferred to the Mount Moriah School District in 1855. The following is an excerpt from the journal of his early teaching days, revealing some of the pitfalls that could befall a teacher at that time—and yet sounding vaguely familiar:

Mr. Combs gave self [Thomas refers to himself in the third person] threatening lecture for

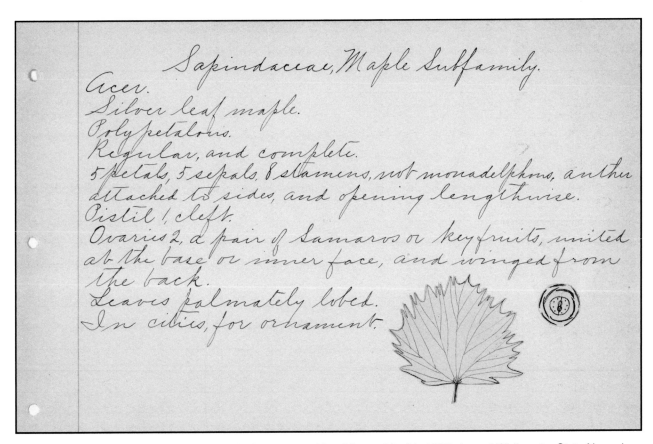

Student Herman C. Westphal made these biology notes with a "dip pen" for his 1895 class at Whitewater State Normal School. He was studying science under Miss Cornelia Rogus.

correcting his child and reminded me of what was done to that schoolteacher in Kentucky. Is he going to inflict the same punishment on me? If so I would better leave. Summer weather, extra intermission for children under six years. Mr. Combs sent his little daughter to school as usual, though he accused me of frightening the child into fits. Is there any fair reasoning in his assertions? Must our school which belongs to the whole district be kept back in their learning to oblige one? When the school is in an uproar, who learns?

Terms were short. In the early days, children attended school for only two months in the fall and two months in late spring, in order to accommodate the planting and harvesting cycles of family farms that required the labor of even the smallest children. Later, five- and six-month terms were similarly divided, until the emergence of automated farm methods permitted the current nine-month school year. Other factors that contributed to longer terms were better heating and maintenance of school buildings, and teachers who became more mobile by riding horses or driving their own cars.

In her essay titled "School," Frances Sprain recalls attending Russell Flats School in Westfield early in the 1900s:

Tardiness and absences were the rule and discipline was a genuine problem. Prudent communities hired a man to teach for the winter months, when the rowdy farm boys were free to come to school, and a woman for the spring term, when the class was made up almost entirely of girls. Teachers usually came from outside the area, but sometimes they were local girls who had their own brothers and sisters as pupils.

All children who attended school walked, regardless of the distance. In winter, their pail lunches would freeze during the walk, so the pails were set by the stove to thaw in time for lunch. During warm weather sessions, it was not unusual for students to abandon their shoes in order to save on leather. Parents bought the textbooks, which usually consisted of an ABC primer, four different readers over the years, two geographies, two histories, a spelling book, and a writing text for the elementary grades. These were passed down from child to child.

Until the 1960s, when the state legislature required that elementary schools must belong to a school district that included a high school, rural children either abandoned their studies after the eighth grade or had to find a way to attend high school in a larger town. This involved long separations from

Courtesy Marathon County Historical Society

These rough and ready football players from Darlington High School demonstrate the longstanding appeal of this popular sport. At the time this photo was taken, only college and professional teams could afford uniforms, and the only safety accessories available were leather helmets and a few thin, carefully positioned pads.

family and friends while they stayed in boarding houses, or with friends of the family or relatives.

Teaching included much more than simple instruction. Very early on, teachers had to sharpen bird quills into pens and fashion other materials such as writing slates and pencils for their students. Male teachers had to chop wood for the stoves, while females enlisted the aid of older male students. Morning duties included lighting the stove, which was used to keep the building warm, dry out wet mittens, and heat soup and hot chocolate for lunch.

Teachers performed building maintenance tasks such as trimming lamp wicks and cleaning glass chimneys; sweeping; washing windows and floors; and enforcing discipline, which could involve a slap (or several) on the back of a child's hand with a ruler, the twist of an ear, or, for more serious infractions, a switching across the back of the legs with a willow branch.

Free Schools for Free Thought

Not surprisingly, the first free school system was the lovingly nurtured brainchild of a German, Michael Frank. He moved to Southport in 1839 at 35 years of age, and became the first village president. When Southport changed its name to Kenosha 11 years later, he became the town's first mayor. Co-founder and editor of the *Southport Telegraph* (with partner Christopher Sholes), Frank stumped in its pages for the establishment of free public schools.

Frank firmly believed in a system of education that provided tuition-free learning for all children, regardless of economic or social class, feeling that education for everyone meant a better life for everyone. If all children had the benefit of education, despite the family's inability to pay, Frank believed they all had better chances of becoming citizens who would contribute to society. In 1841, he started a group called the Free School Friends and carried his fight to the state legislature.

Three separate attempts to introduce statewide legislation were put down by property owners who opposed such taxation as "unadulterated radicalism." Frank then introduced a state bill

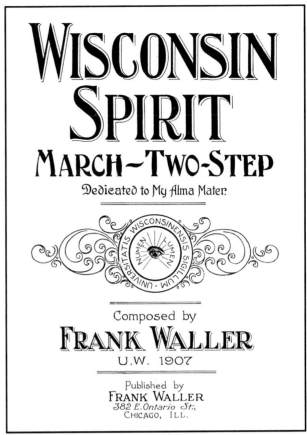

WISCONSIN SPIRIT

MARCH~TWO-STEP

Dedicated to My Alma Mater.

Composed by

FRANK WALLER

U.W. 1907

Published by
FRANK WALLER
382 E. Ontario St.,
CHICAGO, ILL.

Despite its shaky beginning, the University of Wisconsin went on to become the pride of the state. U-W graduate Frank Waller was inspired to compose this piece of two-step march music, dedicated to his alma mater.

pertaining only to Southport, one that would tax its citizens to support a free school in the community.

A meeting of 170 local citizens was held in 1845 to decide the free school question. One wealthy citizen, who could afford to send his children to private schools, revealed his contempt for those beneath his own social status by proclaiming, "What? I to be taxed to pay for the education of the damn Dutch and Irish? Never!"

His sentiment was countered by the remarks of a more community-minded resident:

> Yes! You and I and all of us should be taxed for schools in which our children and the children of the Dutch and Irish immigrants may be given an education which will help in making them, let us hope, better citizens than you and I are.

At that April meeting in Southport, free schools were endorsed by a margin of eleven ballots, which started the ball rolling toward a statewide public school system. Frank later did for high schools what he had done for elementary schools, and so the first free high school was established in Kenosha in 1849. By the end of the Civil War, tuition-free high schools were established in the towns of Fond du Lac, Green Bay, Janesville, La Crosse, Madison, Milwaukee, Prairie du Chien, and Watertown. Requirements that all Wisconsin land be zoned into school districts were not fully in place until 1962, however, and most rural areas were without their own high schools until then.

Post-Secondary Progress

The University of Wisconsin was incorporated in 1848, becoming an integral part of the state's public education system as mandated by the constitutional charter. It opened in 1849, but the school received no appropriations from the state until 1872. For 23 years, it was entirely dependent on the sale of school lands for support. With only this precarious source of funding, the college nearly collapsed during the wild land speculation that ended in the panic of 1857, when many farm mortgages were called in by Eastern investors. The Civil War also had a devastating effect on the school.

What is now the U-W campus encompassed Camp Randall, a 53½ acre tract named after wartime governor Alexander W. Randall. Originally privately owned, it was turned over to the state in 1861 for use as a military training camp. It became the largest staging area for Wisconsin fighting men, 70,000 of whom passed through on their way to the bloody battlegrounds of the South. Camp Randall included a hospital and a stockade for Confederate prisoners of war. Ironically, while the war contributed much to the college's social stature by highlighting it as a provider of manpower at the front, it demanded so many of Wisconsin's young men that student enrollment dropped, further eroding the school's educational and financial success.

To receive funding under the terms of the 1864 Morrill Land Grant Act, which assisted the states in establishment of land-grant colleges, the

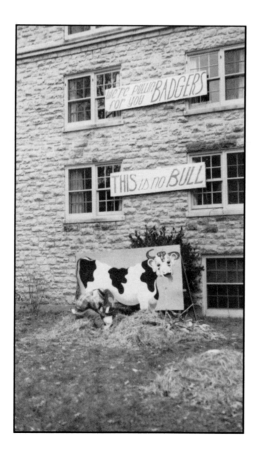

Homecoming in November of 1947. The University of Wisconsin's football tradition includes a longstanding rivalry with Iowa.

An idyllic scene from academia: the University of Wisconsin campus in the spring of 1948.

institution added agricultural, mechanical, and military training courses, which finally put Camp Randall to work for the school in a tangible way. Four years later, 100 women were formally admitted to the college. When it received its first state grant in 1872, a new era had begun.

Left to its own resources, the school had barely been able to sustain itself as a small liberal arts college by implementing innovative approaches to education. For example, it was the first in the state to offer correspondence courses. But under the guidance of president John Bascom (1874-1887), the college grew and established an impressive reputation.

An agricultural experiment station was founded in 1883, from which emerged the Babcock butterfat test, a methodology eventually used by many state auditors to standardize fat content in dairy products. A winter short course for farmers was implemented in 1885, to introduce more scientifically proven methods of agriculture. With the expansion of technical and graduate studies in the 1890s, the institution was transformed from a college into a university, culminating in the creation of the graduate school for political science and history.

This graduate school was headed by Richard T. Ely and, according to a publication of the WPA Writer's Program, *Wisconsin: A Guide To The Badger State* (1941), this department was primarily responsible for establishing the University of Wisconsin's reputation for liberalism, despite the fact that 90 percent of the faculty were regarded as conservative. Ely was investigated for subversive activity in 1894, following labor trouble caused by the depression that year. He was exonerated of any wrongdoing by the school's Board of Regents, and the words of their statement were adopted as the University of Wisconsin's motto:

> Whatever may be the limitations which trammel inquiry elsewhere, we believe that the great State University of Wisconsin should ever encourage that continual and fearless sifting and winnowing by which alone the truth can be found.

Another early manifestation of progressive thought was the founding of the Milwaukee Female

U-W students head for home via the rails in 1910.

Seminary in September of 1848 by Mrs. William Parsons, wife of a Congregational minister. The institution was located at the corner of Milwaukee and Wells streets, and was chartered by the state legislature in 1851—a time when colleges for women were virtually unheard of.

But there was another such institution, Downer College, located in Fox Lake. It ran into financial difficulties in 1895, and merged with Milwaukee Female Seminary to become Milwaukee Downer College. The school became more secular, and relocated to the corner of East Hartford and North Downer avenues. It later served as a teacher's college (Milwaukee Normal School), and was purchased by the University of Wisconsin-Milwaukee in 1964.

Teaching the Teachers

The 1857 legislature set aside one-quarter of the proceeds from a federal land grant to create a fund for the establishment of "normal schools." The first such school was established at Platteville in 1866; another opened in Whitewater two years later. Next came schools in Oshkosh, River Falls, Milwaukee, Stevens Point, Superior, La Crosse, and Eau Claire, the last of which opened in 1916.

Initially, the normal schools differed from most universities and colleges in that they were authorized to provide only two years of college-level work, and women were allowed to attend. In 1927 these schools were upgraded and allowed to offer bachelor of education degrees. They were then called state teacher's colleges, and their graduates generally went on to teach in cities and more populous areas.

In 1887, Marathon County School Superintendent John La Mont urged State Senator A. L. Kruetzer to introduce legislation addressing the need for training of rural teachers. Until then, there were no standards for those who were educating children

Rules of Conduct for a Teacher

The following rules governing the conduct of a (female) schoolteacher originally appeared in a school bulletin in 1915. Their harsh infringement upon the private life of a teacher makes the job sound more like a prison sentence than a profession, but such was the life that a mentor of children was expected to lead:

1. You will not marry during the term of your contract.

2. You are not to keep company with men.

3. You must be at home between the hours of 8 p.m. and 6 a.m. unless attending a school function.

4. You may not loiter downtown in ice-cream stores.

5. You may not travel beyond the city limits unless you have the permission of the chairman of the board.

6. You may not ride in a carriage or automobile with any man unless he is your father or brother.

7. You may not smoke cigarettes.

8. You may not dress in bright colors.

9. You may under no circumstances dye your hair.

10. You must wear at least two petticoats.

11. Your dresses must not be shorter than two inches above the ankle.

12. To keep the schoolroom neat and clean, you must:
    - Sweep the floor at least once daily
    - Scrub the floor at least once a week with hot, soapy water
    - Clean the blackboards at least once a day
    - Start the fire at 7 a.m. so the room will be warm by 8 a.m.

in rural areas, sometimes resulting in a noticeable dichotomy between the skill levels of city children and their country counterparts.

In a pilot program, the Marathon County Board appropriated $12,000 for a building, which was completed in October of 1902. It housed the Training School for Teachers and the Training School for Agriculture and Domestic Economy. Before the building was completed, classes began in Wausau's Humboldt School in September of 1899. The school had 48 faculty members. The principal's salary was a generous $1,800 annually, and the average teacher made $1,300. The school ultimately graduated 1,444 teachers, most of whom went on to teach in 365 rural Wisconsin schools.

In 1949, the state teacher's colleges began to offer bachelor of arts degrees, and by 1951 they were renamed Wisconsin state colleges. In a joint effort with the University of Wisconsin, the 1955 legislature consolidated these schools under a single coordinating committee, while each school maintained a separate board of regents. This allowed each college to retain its local flavor and special strengths while joining a system that established budgets, set priorities for new construction, determined educational programs, and planned the interaction of existing facilities and staff. The result was the University of Wisconsin system, which remains one of the most highly regarded systems of higher education in the country.

BADGER PROFILE: Champion of Kindergarten

Margarethe Meyer Schurz
1833-1876

Margarethe Meyer was born on August 27, 1833, into a prosperous Jewish manufacturing and merchant family in Hamburg, Germany, where she was encouraged to pursue her interest in the arts, education, and liberal thought. At age 16, she attended lectures given by Friedrich Froebel, founder of the kindergarten movement.

"Kindergarten" was a term given by Froebel to his idea of a nurturing atmosphere in which children could be cultivated to grow as flowers do in a garden. In such a progressive setting, children learned social interaction and enhanced their motor skills by participating in games and songs and using various play materials before going to formal school classes.

In 1852, Meyer traveled to London to care for a sick sister and to help her maintain an experimental kindergarten—the first in England. Here she met Carl Schurz, who had come to London after being expelled from Germany. After a brief courtship, they were married in July and emigrated

that fall to America. In poor health following the birth of their first child, Margarethe returned with her husband to England in 1855 for a period of convalescence. They settled the following year in Watertown, Wisconsin.

In the winter of 1857, Margarethe used one of the rooms in their new house as a small kindergarten to teach her daughter Agathe and several of the neighbor children according to the system established by Froebel. An acquaintance then introduced the kindergarten idea back in her hometown of St. Louis, Missouri, where it was incorporated into the public school system.

In 1859, Agathe was introduced to Elizabeth Peabody, an educator from Boston. Ms. Peabody watched Agathe's calming effect on her own four lively children and remarked, "Mrs. Schurz, that child of yours is a miracle, so child-like and unconscious and yet so wise and able, attracting and ruling the other children who seem nothing short of enchanted."

"No miracle," Margarethe explained. "Just brought up in a kindergarten."

Peabody, a reform enthusiast, was impressed, and promptly founded her own formal kindergarten in Boston the following year. Margarethe Schurz encouraged this movement by sending Peabody the preface to Froebel's *Education of Man*. She also spread the word about the new early childhood education when she accompanied her husband on his political travels.

Despite her energetic nature, Margarethe continued to suffer from ill health for the rest of her life. After the birth of their fifth child, Margarethe traveled to Germany in order to recuperate. Upon returning in 1876, she died at the family home in New York on March 15. She was just 42 years old, but she had left a legacy of new ideas that would continue to influence American education for centuries.

BADGER PROFILE: A Voice for Freedom

Carl Schurz was born in Liblar, Germany, on March 2, 1829. As a young man, he attended the University of Bonn as a doctoral candidate in history. A passionate idealist, he became at 19 the leader of a student movement that eventually spearheaded the revolution against despotic Kaiser Frederick Wilhelm IV.

The Kaiser, in an effort to appease the ruling military caste in Prussia, abolished the liberal National Assembly and substituted a conservative cabinet of his own choosing. He reinstituted an almost feudal system of landlord/tenant rule. Those who suffered most acutely were Poles and Slavs who came under Prussian rule after the Congress of Vienna, following Napoleon Bonaparte's 1815 defeat at Waterloo. Intellectuals and politicians who spoke against the Kaiser were arrested and thrown in prison on trumped-up charges supported by perjured police testimony.

Schurz, along with thousands of his countrymen, wanted to see military dictatorship replaced by democratic rule. In 1849, he was commissioned a lieutenant in the illegal revolutionary army. When the revolutionaries were defeated by the Prussian army, Schurz fled the country, knowing he would be executed for treason if captured. He went to Paris, where he became involved in newspaper work and teaching activities.

In one of the most daring exploits of the revolution, he later returned to Germany using a false passport. There, he managed to rescue a professor from the notorious Spandau prison and smuggle him out of the country as well. After a short residence in England, Schurz migrated to the United States in 1852, and settled in Philadelphia. Three years later he moved to Watertown, Wisconsin, where he immediately became involved in the anti-slavery movement.

Schurz also got involved in state politics, running unsuccessfully for lieutenant governor in 1857. Though he failed to gain the post, he had estab-

Courtesy Wisconsin State Historical Society

Carl Schurz

1829-1906

lished his reputation as a powerful orator and a man of ideas. After studying law, he was admitted to the bar and set up a legal practice in Milwaukee in 1859. Schurz' militant liberal politics and his reform-minded ideals led him to become chairman of the Wisconsin delegation of the newly formed Republican Party. That post took him to the convention in 1860, and from the floor he strongly supported Abraham Lincoln for the presidential seat.

Schurz' persuasive speaking skills made him a valuable asset in Lincoln's campaign, during which he succeeded in luring his fellow German-Americans from the Democratic Party to Republican allegiance. This was no small coup, for the considerable sway imparted by the German-born voters was crucial to Lincoln's upstart run against established anti-abolitionist Stephen Douglas. In appreciation for his service, the new president appointed Schurz minister to Spain in 1861.

Schurz was grateful for the recognition, but wished instead to serve in the Union forces that were just beginning to clash with the Army of the Confederacy in the aftermath of the firing on Fort Sumter. Lincoln commissioned him a brigadier-general of volunteers, and Schurz was assigned to General Fremont's Virginia division in 1862. He was promoted to major general the following year, and he served in this capacity until his resignation in 1865.

Schurz returned to Wisconsin after the war, but he stayed only a short time. In 1867, he moved first to Detroit, Michigan, then to St. Louis, Missouri. He became editor of the *Westliche Post,* a leading German-language newspaper. He served one term as a Missouri senator before moving to the East Coast to serve as Secretary of the Interior in the Rutherford B. Hayes administration. By 1881, he had returned to journalism as editor of the *New York Evening Post,* and as a regular contributor to *Harper's Weekly.* For three years, beginning in 1892, Schurz served as president of the National Civil Service Reform League. He died at his New York home on May 14, 1906.

Chapter Four

MAKING IT WORK

The excitement of new settlement was tempered by the realities of everyday life—mouths to feed, bills to pay, work to do. Earning a living in early Wisconsin was done in a variety of ways. Agriculture has always been a staple of the Badger State's economy, but there were other industries developing in Wisconsin. Manufacturing, railroading, forestry, shipping, and the dairy industry all thrived in a state whose natural resources were just beginning to surface.

By the Sweat of Our Brows

By the time the 1870s arrived, Wisconsin had become the leading wheat-producing state in the Union. Other early crops included potatoes, peas, rutabagas, and various staples that required little processing for table use. Grass crops such as hay and alfalfa were grown to support livestock.

There was no supply of fresh milk before the first dairy cows arrived here in 1845 at Big Bull Falls

Publishers of Wausau's weekly newspaper, the *Central Wisconsin,* pose in front of their office building on Jackson Street in 1873. The man on the balcony sporting a "stove pipe" hat is R.H. Johnson, editor of the paper.

Courtesy Marathon County Historical Society

The J.I. Case Company began in Wisconsin as the first maker of portable steam engines. The company grew into a mighty industrial giant when agricultural demand for its machines increased. Here, blacksmiths from the steam engine department pause in their labors for a portrait in 1900.

(later Wausau). These "bovine emigrants" were mostly mongrel Guernseys. At the time, prosperous farmers would generously lend out their full-breed bulls for stud service. It wasn't until the 1890s that forward-looking farmers brought in registered breeds. In some areas, cows were allowed to graze and roam freely until they began to trample and eat the fashionable flower gardens in towns, which led to evening curfews for wandering cattle.

Eventually, as a surplus of dairy goods began to emerge, creameries and cheese factories sprang up, signaling the beginning of a true dairy industry. Dairying was proposed as an alternative to the dying wheat farming industry in the 1850s. It became common in the southeast and south central part of the state within 10 years, as farmers accepted the concept of "single-purpose cows." Previously, subsistence-level farming had required that cows be used for milk, for beef, and as beasts of burden. Once their attitudes shifted, farmers began applying scientific methods of selective breeding, feeding, and herd management to their operations, and a more businesslike eye was cast on their activities. The new methods soon paid off. Wisconsin boasted 245,000 dairy cows by 1867, a number that would increase by tenfold within 45 years.

In 1890, the Milwaukee Railway and Light Company ran this horse-drawn streetcar along National Avenue and Walnut Street. Fare was a nickel per passenger, one-way.

Cheese factories had absorbed most home operations by the 1870s, and corporate enterprises eclipsed home butter producers by the 1890s. By 1907, Wisconsin produced nearly half of the nation's total cheese output, and one- tenth of its butter. "America's Dairyland" had grown up in just over half a century.

Ginseng became a popular cash crop in Wisconsin, where it grew wild over much of the state. The wild ginseng supply was subsequently almost exhausted due to poor management, so most of today's ginseng crop is domesticated. Wisconsin ginseng was first transported to China in the late

1800s, and it has been a substantial trade item since that time.

Another common harvest was that of maple sap for the syrup industry, which reached its zenith in the 1800s but died out (except for a few small operations) by the turn of the century.

Large families were common on farms—as many as 18 children who were essentially raised as free labor. Hired farmhands made about $30 per summer month, including room and board. That dropped by about half in winter, when there was less work to be done. During the Depression, the

The switch engine's crew poses for a photographer in Wausau, about 1890.

John Schlaefer of Wausau (at register) and his brother Mick (not pictured) owned Schlaefer's Bakery at Fifth and Forest streets in 1908. Business was supplemented by the sale of a number of staple goods, displayed on shelves behind the counter. Lighting was provided by gas, but electricity would soon prevail.

figure dropped to $5 for those fortunate enough to find work.

Although certain trades that originally served the agriculture industry—such as blacksmithing and harnessmaking—went into decline with the advent of heavy machinery, other businesses sprang up to take their places, among them engine repair shops and implement stores.

Industry Comes of Age

The Industrial Revolution was in full swing by the time Wisconsin was becoming heavily settled. Forestry and mining were already established. After the virgin forests had been cleared and

replanted, the days of crosscuts and swampers came to an end, paving the way for the mechanized harvesting of second-growth timber by huge paper conglomerates.

Industries grew up around other resources. Ice harvesting was big business in both rural and urban areas, due to the abundance of natural waterways around the state. Before the days of refrigeration, one Milwaukee company employed 1,000 men each winter to saw off rectangular blocks of ice, float them to the warehouse, and pack them in sawdust and marsh hay. When the local warehouses were full, freight trains were loaded and the ice was transported as far south as New Orleans.

By the 1920s, canneries were springing up in central Wisconsin. In the '30s, Central Wisconsin Canneries merged with the Minnesota Valley Canning Company. The new company set up the first mechanized corn-canning line, and took over production from the older Fox Lake Company when its plant burned down. In the early 1950s, the firm came to be known as the Green Giant Company, now one of the most well-known names in the food industry.

The abundance of necessary crops enabled many breweries to start up, particularly in the southeastern part of the state. Because of its location on one of the Great Lakes' most navigable natural ports, its proximity to fresh ingredients, and its large German population with a beer-making heritage, Milwaukee became home to most major American breweries.

Neighborhoods in that city took advantage of the ready availability of their favorite malt beverage. In the 1890s, before beer was bottled, neighbors often chipped in to buy a keg, then filled their own bottles for home use. This was referred to as

Courtesy Milwaukee County Public Library

By 1880, Milwaukee was a major shipping port, and tall-masted ships were often moored in the harbor or at corporate piers jutting into the Milwaukee River.

Normington Bros. Launderers was founded in Stevens Point in 1903. This driver, William Older, delivered laundry in central Wisconsin for about 50 years. The photo was taken in the 1930s.

Larry Mishkar Collection

The Ward House Hotel served travelers passing through Clintonville. It was serviced by a "bus" that was provided by the Four Wheel Drive Auto Company as a convenience to guests.

"rushing the growler." At many Milwaukee industrial plants, a "bucket boy" was sent to the nearest saloon for beer, in order to slake the thirst of those on morning and afternoon breaks.

Later, Wisconsin companies like Heil and A.O. Smith began manufacturing heavy equipment. The Harley Davidson Company was producing "Milwaukee Iron," a nickname given their popular motorcycles by fond enthusiasts as early as 1903.

The hospitality trade invigorated the economy with such businesses as hotels, inns, and restaurants, a Wisconsin tradition that lives on. In particular, the concept of the "supper club" became popular in the state. These establishments combined a working tavern with informal to up-scale dining. The idea probably derived from the German "wursthaus," where a family could enjoy plentiful, tasty food along with Dad's favorite beer. In some supper clubs, entertainment was added in the form of live musicians or a jukebox.

Inns and hotels often took on the air of the country from which their proprietors hailed. In the northern part of the state, boarding houses for loggers evolved into hotels with a distinctly Scandinavian flavor. Wade House, located in Clintonville on the plank road between Sheboygan and Fond du Lac, offered an atmosphere of refinement and intellectual conversation influenced by its New Englander host, Sylvanus Wade. It catered to the stagecoaches that brought travelers from the East, and Abraham Lincoln is said to have enjoyed a hearty meal there on one of his trips through the area.

Milwaukee's Commission Row was established in 1894 between E. Buffalo and E. St. Paul on Broadway, and still serves as the city's wholesale produce district.

Edgar, Wisconsin, established Rural Free Delivery mail service in 1903. By 1906, Henry Piehl was the area's regular letter carrier on Route One, delivering with the aid of his oversized leather bag and a horse-drawn buggy. Henry obviously took his job as a representative of the U.S. Postal Service quite seriously, and dressed accordingly.

Public Servants

By 1870, there were 1,228 post offices serving more than a million people in Wisconsin, according to the census. Rural Free Delivery was established in 1896, effectively cutting the need for so many individual post offices. Previously, anyone living outside of a town had to travel to the nearest town's post office and pick up their mail from a box. With RFD, mail carriers delivered the letters and packages directly to boxes posted along the roads in front of businesses and residences. Even outlying farms now received mail efficiently, and news traveled much faster.

Sanitation in rural areas consisted mainly of what families could arrange for themselves. Burning was one way of getting rid of unwanted flammable refuse. Other items, such as tin cans and bottles, might be buried in a pit. Very large pieces, including appliances and automobiles, were disposed of in less environmentally sound ways—by dumping them over a hill into a bog, for example, or simply by leaving them to rot in the woods. City and town sanitation was normally handled by city crews with wagons or trucks that hauled the trash to landfills.

Law enforcement was of a transient nature until towns grew large enough to support their own police forces. Federal marshals were assigned to larger outposts, but small towns had to hire their own peacekeepers. The job generally fell to anyone who was able and willing to do it.

In 1898, Kenosha's police department consisted of six patrol officers and the chief. Milwaukee's first police force, established in 1906, also boasted six officers. They were each paid $40 per month, and during that first year the officers investigated six burglaries and one murder. In 1929, Milwaukee introduced mounted traffic cops. The mounted officers customarily stopped so that citizens could

In the 1890s, Wausau's police force consisted of the chief and six officers. Note the resemblance of the uniforms to those worn by Union officers during the Civil War and by the U.S. Cavalry, which still used horses for mounts at the time of this photo.

feed the horses lumps of sugar, carrots, or the occasional apple—an effective public relations policy.

Kenosha introduced a federal lifesaving station in 1879, a precursor to the Coast Guard. The crew of eight made $40 per month in payment for their efforts to aid drowning swimmers and overturned or floundering vessels, small pay for what can be heroic effort in the large swells of Lake Michigan.

Firefighting crews at the turn of the century were a glorious lot. They charged to fires atop coal-fired, horse-drawn pumper wagons that used steam to power the pumps. These shiny new devices were a far cry from the days of bucket brigades and wet blankets. With their warning bells clanging, boiler belching black smoke, hoofs clattering along the cobblestones, and whips cracking over the backs of the horses, the engines were used to save lives and burning buildings. Firemen were the heroes of every small boy.

Harold Gauer, Milwaukee author and historian, recalls his excitement as a young boy running alongside the noisy cavalcade of firefighting equipment:

A Milwaukee fire engine races to the scene of an 1890s blaze, steam churning out the stack of the gleaming brass boiler rig and hooves clattering over the cobbled streets. Unlike many fire departments, this one obviously chose horses for their speed, not their beauty.

Men clung to the side rails with one hand, struggling into oilskins with the other arm. Those with seats desperately tugged on their rubber boots. The chap in charge of the bell kept ringing it with frantic diligence. It was pure spectacle, and it surely attracted an appreciative following.

However, the life of a fireman wasn't all noise and excitement. Firemen kept the ever-present boiler rig fire going, tended to the horses, cared for the firehouse itself, and cooked meals for the crew.

After a fire, they had to scrape the hot coals from the boiler onto a brick-paved ramp outside the firehouse, hang the hoses from the tower to dry, and clean and shine the engine. But when the fire bell rang again, they jumped into their gear, slid down brass poles to the waiting rigs, hitched up the matched-stallion team, and set off for the site of the blaze. Once again, they were white knights off to fight the evil fire, and almost every boy knew in his heart that someday he, too, would be a fireman.

Cape's Street Grading Machine Cor. Center

Milwaukee's Public Works Department grades new streets in 1907. Businesses outside of agriculture had by this time discovered many uses for J.I. Case's portable steam engine. One of the black iron behemoths works here alongside horse teams, a fitting visual metaphor for the rapidly evolving industrial scene.

BADGER PROFILE: Wisconsin's Greatest Son

Robert La Follette
1855-1925

Robert Marion La Follette, Sr. was born on June 14, 1855, of French immigrant parents who had settled on a farm in the Dane County township of Primrose. He entered the University of Wisconsin in 1874. He distinguished himself as an orator and as editor of the campus newspaper, and graduated with his bachelor's degree in legal studies in 1879. He was admitted to the bar the following year.

In 1880, La Follette entered the political scene in a big way, challenging the entrenched political machine of Republican "boss" Elisha Keyes. Although Keyes' only official position was Postmaster of the Madison post office, he ran an "underground" system of graft and corruption that had infiltrated all levels of government, a Wisconsin version of New York's Boss Tweed and Tammany Hall.

La Follette, undaunted by Keyes' ruthless reputation, beat the odds by riding his old mare, Gypsy, across the countryside and stumping for his own idealistic views. At 25 years old, "Fighting Bob"

won the Republican Party's nomination and then the office of Dane County District Attorney by 93 votes, despite Keyes' determined opposition. The mold had been cast.

Throughout his busy political life, La Follette would continue to be a thorn in the side of the established Republican Party, making a name for himself as a progressive reformer. He thwarted the plans of lumber, railroad, and corporate barons to exploit the resources found on Indian lands, much to the chagrin of the barons' corrupt friends within the party. La Follette's ideals caused a rift that eventually split the Republicans into two factions, the stalwarts and the progressives.

Four years after his Dane County victory, La Follette won a seat in Congress and held onto it for three terms. In the election of 1890, a Democratic sweep removed him from that seat and returned him to private law practice. When La Follette was offered a bribe by Senator Philetus Sawyer, who was facing trial for taking kickbacks, to help sway the opinion of Circuit Court Judge Robert Siebecker (La Follette's brother-in-law), La Follette was so outraged that he once again became involved in politics.

He sought the office of governor in 1896, but was unable to overcome bribes offered by stalwarts to convention delegates. The same thing happened in 1898, but La Follette had by then gained enough political momentum to influence the party platform on his own. He instituted a plank for reform in railroad usage by public officials, which disallowed the common practice of free passes for government employees. Railroads had been using the passes as a means of buying legislative votes. Planks were also approved to establish an income tax on corporations and direct primary elections for the nomination of political candidates. Many progressive acts were passed during Governor Edward Scofield's administration, most at the insistence of La Follette.

In 1900, with the aid of a financial backer and an exhaustive speaking campaign, La Follette finally gained the governor's seat. He was re-elected in 1902 and 1904. The many reforms implemented during his terms included the establishment of a Tax Commission, a Railroad Commission, a Civil Service Commission, and the State Board of Forestry. He aided passage of bills establishing a life insurance regulatory code, a state income tax, a corrupt practices act, and commissions on conservation and industry.

Perhaps La Follette's biggest contribution as governor was his creation of a "brain trust," whereby he appointed experts and specialists from the University of Wisconsin to state boards and commissions, in the belief that a state should benefit from its best minds. The practice came to be known as the "Wisconsin Idea," and was copied by later progressive governors, by other states, and by the federal government.

La Follette went on to serve in the U.S. Senate, and was instrumental in the passage of federal reform bills similar to those he had shepherded through the Wisconsin legislature. He forwarded or worked on behalf of bills regulating employer liability, protecting workers, overseeing interstate commerce, and reforming the banking industry.

He was well-liked by other reform-minded activists such as Gifford Pinchot, future father of the U.S. Forest Service, who filled in on the campaign trail in 1910 when La Follette was too ill to make the rounds on his own behalf. La Follette served as a senator from 1905 until his death in 1925. Because of his strong, progressive ideas and his moral steadfastness, he became known in political circles as the conscience of the Republican Party.

Robert La Follette's portrait hangs in the United States Senate lounge, commemorating his career as one of the five most outstanding senators in America's history. His sculpted likeness also graces Statuary Hall in the nation's capitol, venerating him as Wisconsin's greatest son.

POLITICAL MARKET

CONSCIENTIOUS RAIL-ROAD PRESIDENT TO DEALER. *"Ah! let me see. I think I'll take this bunch of Legislators at $5000 a head. The Senators, at—what price did you say?"*

DEALER. *"Can't afford 'em less than $10,000 each."*

R. R. P. *"Well, hand them over. I suppose I'll have to take the lot."*

DEALER. *"Any thing else to-day? I have a lot of Editors, at various prices, from a Thousand down to Fifty Cents."*

R. R. P. *"No, nothing in that way, to-day. But I want a Governor very much indeed, and will stand $50,000 for him. Get me a Wisconsin one, if possible!"*

Harper's Weekly addressed the issue of corrupt politicians— a problem that was the target of many La Follette reforms—in this editorial cartoon from the June 12, 1858 edition.

BADGER PROFILE: Attorney, Advisor, Activist

Courtesy State Historical Society of Wisconsin

Belle Case La Follette
1859-1931

The La Follette legacy is one that continues to influence America. No other senator had as much impact on economic and humanitarian reforms in the nation. He fought diligently for his ideals, and devoted his life to the belief that government should truly be of the people, by the people, and for the people. Robert Marion La Follette, Sr. lived his life around his belief that "the will of the people shall be the law of the land."

Belle Case was born in Baraboo, Wisconsin, in 1859. She attended the University of Wisconsin, and there met Robert La Follette. The two graduated in the same year, and when Robert became county district attorney in 1881, they were married. Four years later, Belle became the first woman to receive a degree from the university's law school.

Belle never practiced law, but she was her husband's most valuable political and legal advisor. He acknowledged in later years that she was "altogether the brainiest member of my family . . . Her

grasp of the great problems, sociological and economic, is unsurpassed by any of the strong men who have been associated with me in my work."

Belle was a great influence on her husband as he fought for the rights of blacks, for women's suffrage, and for pacifism. These were all ideas that Belle strongly advocated. Her activism and influence as a political wife were not equaled until the Roosevelt administration, when Eleanor served as primary advisor to her husband Franklin in the White House, after the torch of progressivism had been passed from the Republicans to the Democratic Party.

Not limited solely to her husband's political activities, Belle pursued her own interests with zeal. Seeing clearly the war clouds gathering on Europe's horizon, she became involved with the National Council for the Prevention of War and the International League for Peace and Freedom. Like her husband, she was ahead of her time in calling for "an international tribunal which shall make future wars unnecessary and ultimately impossible," pre-dating Woodrow Wilson's League of Nations by nearly five years. Unfortunately, all of these words and efforts failed to prevent the occurrence of World War I.

In 1909, Belle became the first "Home and Educational" editor of *La Follette's Weekly Magazine,* an organ of the progressive movement for 38 years. It espoused the ideas of La Follette and his followers concerning governmental reform and progressive thinking. In 1948, the year after it ceased publication for financial reasons, it was taken over by a Madison non-profit group, and it is published today under the banner of *The Progressive.*

Upon her husband's death in June of 1925, Belle was invited to become a candidate to fill his unexpired Senate term, but she declined. She realized her chances of filling the partial term were good, but that re-election for a woman was unlikely. Not wishing to waste the political capital of Robert Sr.'s memory, she chose instead to throw her influence behind a political career for her son, Robert M., Jr. Her selflessness paid off, as "Young Bob" won his father's old seat by a landslide and took office in December.

Belle's official reason for not running was that she needed time to herself in order to write her husband's biography. Sadly, the book was only partially completed at the time of her death in 1931.

In 1935, one out-of-work photographer earned his living by going house to house, offering to photograph children atop his patient pony. This photo was purchased for 50 cents in the town of Lake, Wisconsin.

Chapter Five

A TIME FOR PLAY

Between the resourcefulness of the people and the endless possibilities offered by the land itself, there was no shortage of recreation and pleasure for early Wisconsinites. With typical enthusiasm, they played as hard as they worked.

Fun and Games in the Heartland

By the end of the 1800s, revolutionary changes were afoot in the working world. The introduction of the ten-hour workday, Saturday half-holidays, and the two-week summer vacation allowed Wisconsinites to begin experiencing the luxury of leisure time. Previously, the workday had been as long as 16 hours, with a six-day work week. There were no time-saving devices such as automatic washing machines or fast automobiles to allow more leisure time.

Taking advantage of progress, people began coming up with new ways to enjoy their off-work hours. Most of today's spectator sports were founded between the end of the Civil War and the turn of the century. Basketball, for example, was introduced in the 1890s by Dr. James Naismith. It was first played with two nine-man teams, and peach baskets were used for goals. The sport

Dressed for a dip: These Milwaukee women are summering at Lake Okauchee in Waukesha County, about 1915.

Courtesy Ralph Wehlitz

Heading "Up North" for a week of stalking the regal whitetail is a time-honored Wisconsin tradition. Aside from the clothing and weapons, this late 1800s deer camp could be one found in today's great northwoods.

Formal tennis attire in Milwaukee, early 1900s.

immediately caught on and drew excited crowds wherever it was played. The American penchant for team competition had begun.

Victorian ideals were still prevalent, but fun in the guise of healthy exercise was acceptable, and athletic crazes swept the country. Croquet, a game requiring strategic skill and yet polite enough for the ladies, became a virtual epidemic. Begun on fashionable, manicured lawns in the East, it traveled west with the homesteaders and soon became the game of choice for society's upper crust. In fact, it became so popular that some sets were manufactured with candle sockets attached to the wickets, to allow for nighttime play.

Bicycles, invented in 1816, were all the rage by the "Gay Nineties." Many cyclists carried squirt guns

Smartly dressed women and men spent leisurely afternoons canoeing on the Milwaukee River in 1895. Such outdoor activities were all the rage for city dwellers, many of whom may have imagined themselves the quintessential "Gibson Girl" or "Gibson Man," dressing and posturing like the characters in newspaper drawings by popular illustrator Charles Dana Gibson.

filled with ammonia to repel any vicious dogs they might encounter along the way.

Tennis became popular in the early 1900s. However, shorts weren't considered acceptable clothing for either gender, so men wore baggy pants and white shirts with neckties, while women played in floor-length skirts and shirtwaists. Almost all sports attire was formal. Lawn bowling and golf were also considered to be gentrified enough for the upper classes. Ladies and men alike frequently formed gymnastic societies. In Milwaukee, the Germans founded their social club, *Turnverein,* on gymnastics, and it survives as the present-day Turner's Club.

Wisconsin's varied landscape has always allowed the enjoyment of many outdoor activities. As is the case today, fishing and canoeing were popular in most areas, but especially in the northern regions, where lakes and rivers abound. Hiking was a particularly popular pastime on Rib Mountain near Wausau, which was as close to mountaineering as most Wisconsinites would ever get.

The equipment has changed over the years, but Wisconsinites (and their neighbors) have always taken advantage of the state's vast natural beauty by camping in the woods. Here, a boy enjoys an open-air breakfast in 1914.

The Milwaukee Press Club's annual picnic in 1912 included a dirt-ring boxing match as part of the entertainment.

Hikes were undertaken quite seriously by men and women outfitted in dashing outfits of high-laced leather boots, sporty wool knickers, and silky, velvet-bowed blouses. Any kind of crusher, slouch hat, or modified fedora was acceptable headgear. Male and female canoeists alike opted for the more common straw boater or felt bowler, along with the customary white shirts, pants, dresses, and shoes. Wisconsin's temperate climate also provided enjoyment of winter sports like cross-country and downhill skiing, dogsledding, tobogganing and hockey.

Swimming schools were popular in river towns like Milwaukee, and hapless beginners were often harnessed and dangled from a contraption that resembled a fishing pole, which was controlled by the teacher from a training platform. The device allowed the novice to learn proper strokes and kicking techniques without fear of drowning. Scratchy woolen shorts and tank tops were worn by men and boys, while women were attired in modestly cut bathing suits resembling knee-length dresses. However, it was not uncommon to see country boys belly-flopping into their swimming holes "in the altogether," forsaking the convention of clothing for freedom of movement.

By the 1880s, metal wheels had replaced wooden spool rollers on skates, and children were quick to adopt the faster, more dependable wheels for a spin in the streets, many of which were newly paved. They also spent time on stilts, swings, playing kick-the-can and marbles, flying kites, and viewing new-fangled stereoscopic slides.

Family outings might consist of a steamboat excursion on a nearby lake or a trip to a resort. In summer, a foray to the beach was always a hit. Beaches were often gender-segregated, and people changed into rough wool suits in a public bath house. Small children used air-filled, cloth "water wings" to stay afloat, while older family members sat under large parasols on blankets, guarding baskets of fresh fruit from the thieving hands of youngsters.

City folks had access to public natatoriums— buildings housing large indoor swimming pools that were clean and well-maintained for year-round use. Residents who lacked indoor plumbing frequently went there for a chance to bathe.

In keeping with the formality of Victorian society, even leisure activities required proper dress. For these members of Milwaukee's 1904 "Rough Riders" bowling team, that meant outfits patterned after those worn by Theodore Roosevelt's famed military unit.

Milwaukee's Miller Theater and Hotel, built in 1916, originally hosted vaudeville acts, but was offering "talkies" by the end of the Depression. It was renamed the "Towne" in 1948.

A late 19th-century picnic turns into an impromptu open-air concert by "The Northwestern Band" in Marathon County. In remote areas where there was no opera house or theater, families relied on their own musical talents for entertainment.

Lazy Country Days

Folks who lived in the country also had many ways of entertaining themselves. Often, they hosted relatives or friends who drove out from the cities for a breath of fresh country air. Picnics, barn raisings, and wedding receptions were always good reasons to get together and have some lemonade, fresh cakes, pies, cookies, and lots of hearty farm food.

Wedding receptions usually ended in a "shivaree," with the revelers gathering beneath the newly-weds' bedroom window (honeymoons were unheard of) and making as much noise as possible by shooting guns and setting off blasting caps. Soon, the new groom would appear at the window to "pay off" the noisemakers with some kind of food or other treat. The revelers then returned to the main party until it was time to go home and

milk the cows, an ever-present chore in America's budding Dairyland.

Often, barn raisings ended with a dance inside the new building, where the floor was still clean and free of hay, spilled grain, or animal dung. Those who could play an instrument and were lucky enough to own one assembled themselves into a band, and the barn-raisers danced the night away to the strumming of guitars, the plucking of banjos, and the sawing of a country fiddle. Children played party games like "Button, Button, Who's Got The Button?" and "London Bridge Is Falling Down" until their eyelids got heavy. Then the women tucked them all into bed, visitors along with the residents, until their parents were ready to go home.

The church has traditionally been a center of social

These Milwaukee boys flooded a city backyard and dubbed it "Felsecker's Skating Park" around 1903. Even such strenuous outdoor activity called for proper dress, including the ubiquitous bowler perched jauntily on the skater's head.

activities. To raise needed funds, congregation members held "box socials," picnics for which church women would make box lunches. The meals were auctioned off to the men of the flock. The winning gentleman then received, along with the lunch, the right to share it with the lady who had packed it. Many a country courtship got its start over such a meal.

A trip to town was a chance for the whole family to enjoy a break from the isolation of farmstead life. Women picked out thread and yard goods, and in addition collected a little friendly gossip, fashion tips, and recipes from the ladies in town.

Children ogled the goodies behind the glass case at the drugstore. Husbands took the opportunity to share some drinks and their own brand of gossip at the local watering hole, and the wives would often end up taking the reins for the trip home.

Periodically, a traveling medicine show passed through town. Vaudeville acts would gather the attention of the crowd, then hucksters would attempt (often successfully) to sell their potions, elixirs, and patent medicines. The entertainment value of such events generally outweighed the medicinal benefit to the community.

The Greenbush Public Natatorium was one of several swimming and bathing facilities available in Milwaukee in the early 1900s. They were especially valued by residents who had no indoor plumbing at home.

Floating swimming schools like this one on the Milwaukee River were common in river towns at the turn of the century. Small children learned proper strokes while suspended from a heavy duty "fishing pole."

The Universal Language

Wisconsin settlers brought with them an extraordinary appreciation of music. Early pioneers depended on their own talents for singing, picking and strumming, or visited a town with a theater or opera hall. After the 1877 introduction of the hand-cranked phonograph, prosperous families owned Victrolas that blared out the crackly, wavering, but melodious tones of Caruso and other popular opera stars. An upright piano held a place of honor in some parlors, and families would gather after chores to sing and laugh together.

Traveling minstrels were common by the turn of the century, and stringed duos and trios gave local concerts or played at church and school functions. The musicians often played guitar and mandolin, accompanying a singer who would warble the latest hits and old favorites.

Almost every community had a band, as well as a bandstand designed to accommodate Saturday evening concerts. People strolled past the band-shell to the strains of "Let the Rest of the World Go

By," "In the Shade of the Old Apple Tree," and "Oh, You Beautiful Doll." Hotels held large dances where the participants performed waltzes, one-steps, two-steps, and the Virginia Reel, as well as polkas, square dances, and quadrilles.

Amateur theatricals were staged by high school or college drama clubs, and people of all ages formed literary societies and gave readings. The Young Men's Christian Association was formed at the turn of the century, with facilities in the larger towns that offered healthy recreational opportunities. Those who preferred less "sanctified" activities gathered at billiard halls, where cigars, pipes, and tobacco could be purchased.

Eat, Drink and Be Merry

Wisconsin has long enjoyed a reputation as a bastion of gastronomic delight. The history of Milwaukee parallels this development, so we'll take a look at that city.

In the late 1890s, beer gardens were popular places to spend a night on the town. The Schlitz

84

Palm Garden on Third Street was perhaps the most famous of these. It boasted a high domed ceiling, from which ornate crystal light fixtures dangled. Potted palms, stained glass windows, and rich oil paintings contributed to the exotic atmosphere. House musicians serenaded customers sitting at tables, and on Sunday nights national orchestras were booked as special entertainment. From the beer garden, customers might walk down the street to Mader's or one of the other "up-scale" restaurants for a meal of hearty, Old World food.

By the early part of the 20th century, Milwaukee had licensed 2,440 taverns, 6,767 bartenders, and 2,630 pinball machines. Some northside and southside neighborhoods had five or six taverns on every block. Many were owned by the breweries, and consequently sold only products manufactured by the host company. Taverns had their own distinctive odors–essences of pickled pig's feet, hard-boiled eggs, braunschweiger, sawdust, and spilled beer.

Before 1850, bourbon was sold for 15 cents a gallon, but a law enacted that year taxed whiskey at one dollar per gallon and beer at one dollar per barrel. Beer subsequently became the beverage of choice for thrifty imbibers, furthering shoring up Milwaukee's already thriving brewing industry.

Betting was legal, and Jordan's Cafe posted odds behind the bar for just about any contest one might care to wager on. During the First World War, taverns were opened before dawn to accommodate workers on the graveyard shift in Milwaukee munitions plants.

In the 1930s, one bar served a huge hamburger slathered with barbecue sauce and a plate of shoestring potatoes, a combo referred to as "Texas and Shoes." Wine was five cents a glass, beer a dime, and cocktails went for a quarter.

By the time Harold and Janet DuBois opened a hamburger stand called "The Spot" on Independence Day in 1945, hamburgers cost 20 cents, hot dogs 15 cents, malts were a quarter, and an ice-cream sundae would set you back a cool 20 cents.

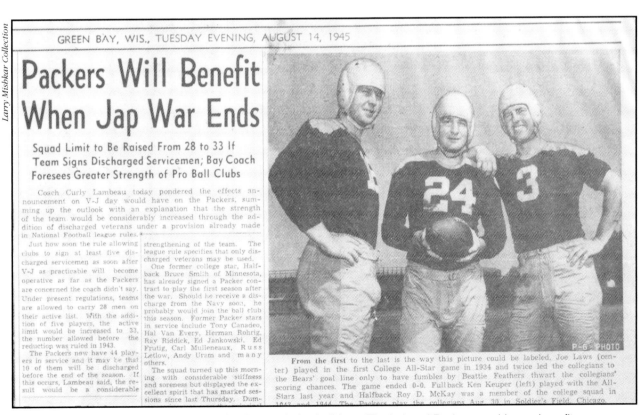

The end of World War II was good news for Wisconsin football fans: The beloved Packers would soon benefit from the return of veterans.

This was the view from the grandstand at Milwaukee's State Fair Park in 1931. A life-size "ship," complete with main mast, sits in the middle ground at left, with what looks like a go-cart race track in front of it. In the foreground, concessionaires offer Old Heidelberg beer and 25-cent plate lunches.

From Stage to Silver Screen

Like many theaters statewide, Milwaukee's Schlitz Park Theatre in the 1890s offered live plays and operas. A theater-in-the-round, the auditorium seated several hundred people and benefited from its location on the north end of the beer garden. The Uihlein Theater offered check rooms for bicycles and four bars where Schlitz beer was sold. It opened in 1896, serving the public for the next 54 years.

In 1904, the Crystal Theater opened as a vaudeville house, presenting the latest New York acts to Milwaukee patrons. The first six rows and box seats went for a dime to 30 cents each. By the 1920s, silent films were replacing vaudeville as the leading form of entertainment, and Milwaukee began its reign as the home of some of the most opulent movie houses in America. Silent films often starred Theda Bara, the actress who invented the "vamp," and who began life as a Milwaukee girl named Theodosia Goodman.

By 1939, "talkies" such as *Ice Follies,* starring Joan Crawford and Jimmy Stewart, and *The Oklahoma Kid* with James Cagney, Humphrey Bogart, and Rosemary Lane were pleasing crowds.

The Roar of the Big Top

The lure of the circus and the excitement of state and county fairs have long been a part of Wisconsin life. County fairs are places to meet friends, play some games, win some prizes, and show off the year's best efforts—preserves, 4-H livestock, artwork, crafts, and more. The Wisconsin State Fair simply provides a larger venue and a chance to measure your community's best against the rest of the state.

This popular institution had its beginnings in Janesville, where the first Wisconsin State Fair was held October 1-2, 1851. The celebration was sponsored by the Wisconsin Agricultural Society, and 13 counties were represented. The fairgrounds covered six acres, and more than 10,000 people flocked to see the exhibitions of horses, sheep, cattle, and swine, plus the newest in farm implements, dairy products, and many of the same attractions that still make the fair such a popular event. That first fair featured an inaugural address by U-W Chancellor John Lathrop and plowing contests pitting adventuresome farmers and their teams against each other.

In 1909, one of the most popular events at the Wisconsin State Fair featured two steam locomotives. The two powerful machines backed down the tracks from each other, worked up a full head of steam, then charged full tilt, creating a spectacular SMASH! at the end. This early demolition derby was a much-publicized spectacle.

Perhaps the biggest crowd-pleaser of all, though, was the circus, a Wisconsin institution since the days before statehood. By 1938, when the last of the native Wisconsin shows closed, more than 100 circuses had debuted in the state. Among the larger shows were the Ringling Brothers, the Mabie Brothers, the Five Gollmars (at one time the third-largest show in the country), the Lindemans, Burr Robins, and William C. Coup.

One rags-to-riches circus story involved Ephraim Williams, Wisconsin's only black circus owner. Initially quite poor, Williams dreamed of the day he would do more than shine white folks' shoes. He saved his money, bought a horse, trained it to do tricks, and made the rounds of Wisconsin theaters with his act. He moved to Appleton in 1885 and bought a partnership in Ferguson and Williams' Monster Shows, which were touring the state.

In 1890, Williams launched his own Medford circus. "Professor Williams' Consolidated American & German Shows" toured for three years before declaring bankruptcy. Williams revived the show in 1901, but it failed again two years later. Undaunted, he joined a tent show run by a New Orleans man, Silas Green.

One night, discouraged by a storm that leveled the tent, Green swore off the circus life and left the whole operation to Williams. The new owner developed the show into a southern institution, introducing such stars as Bessie Smith. Williams' circus thrived until the 1950s.

Delavan was home to 26 circuses; Sparta boasted the Bugler & Chaney Railroad Shows; and Evansville gave us the George W. Hall Show. Birnamwood was headquarters for the Halloway Bros.; Dorchester had Skerbeck's Circus; and the Dode Fish Shows made their home in Wonewoc. Some of the smaller shows that couldn't afford to ride the rails instead traversed dirt roads that could become mucky quagmires after a soaking rain. These enterprises became known as "mud shows." In their caravans, the elephants always traveled at the rear, available to extricate wagons that had become mired in the mud.

Advance men, early masters of public relations, came to town before each show, plastering every available surface with brightly colored posters. By the time the circus actually rolled into town, children had been whipped into such a frenzy of anticipation that they ran alongside the wagons, screaming and jostling for a better view, virtually ensuring SRO attendance at the paid performances.

Ringling Brothers' circus passes through Black River Falls on its way to an August 17, 1883 show. Parades like these were exhaustively promoted by "advance men." You can see the handiwork of these publicity men on the wall at left, which has been plastered from end to end with large posters extolling the bigger-than-life attractions offered by the circus.

Courtesy Black River Falls Historical Society

The Greatest Show On Earth

Phineas T. Barnum wasn't himself a showman. He was proprietor of Barnum's American Museum on Broadway in New York. There he exhibited macabre human oddities and "freaks of nature." His New York museum was a tremendous success, due to Barnum's savvy use of sensational promotional stunts. For instance, he wrote the speech that six-year-old "General Tom Thumb" (billed as "a dwarf of 11 years of age, just arrived from England") gave at his debut in Barnum's lecture hall:

> Good evening, ladies and gentlemen. I am only Thumb, but a good hand in a general way at amusing you, for though I am a mite, I am mighty . . . In short, don't make much of me, for making more would be making me less. Though I grow in your favor, no taller I'd be.

In 1844, audiences lapped up this kind of nonsensical whimsy, and Barnum played the "General's" diminutive stature to the hilt. Undeniably, he had a good head for business, and an even better sense of public relations.

When Bill Coup of Delavan's Coup and Castello Circus came to Barnum in 1870, in search of capital to invest in "the greatest show on earth," Barnum was skeptical, but he listened thoughtfully. He finally agreed to lend his name and a considerable amount of money to the combined venture, which was dubbed "P.T. Barnum's Circus and Museum."

The new show was the largest ever assembled in the Midwest, with huge tents, trapeze and high-wire equipment, and more animals than ever before. By the time it had traveled to New York, Barnum's museum show was added, and

when the first circus train took to the rails in the spring of 1872, a new era of circus history had begun.

Coup split with Barnum over policy differences in 1876. Barnum continued on his own until 1881, when he was joined by James Bailey. Together, they pushed and promoted until their circus was at the forefront of the industry. Barnum died in 1891, and Bailey passed away in 1906. Without capable managers or promoters, the greatest show on earth was soon mired in financial troubles.

Meanwhile, five brothers with the last name of Ringling (an Americanized version of the German name "Rüngeling") had established a popular circus based in Baraboo. After purchasing the Yankee Robinson Show in 1884, they staged their first performance of "Great Double Shows, Circus and Caravan." It

Courtesy Milwaukee Public Library

The Barnum & London Circus parades through the streets of Milwaukee in 1890.

was May of that year, and their big top measured 45 feet by 9 feet. They had no band wagon, and the menagerie wasn't added until two years later.

Like their predecessor Barnum, the Ringlings showed signs of the marketing genius that would mark their entire circus careers. Advertising a new animal act as the "Hideous Hyena Striata Gigantium, the Mammoth, Midnight Marauding, Man-Eating Monstrosity," they reached new heights of hyperbole—and attracted a huge audience of curiosity seekers. By 1890, they had graduated from being pulled by rented farm horses to riding the rails with the "big boys." When they were audacious enough to enter the domain of rival circuses in the East, they weren't taken seriously because they refused to allow "grifters"—bunco artists, short-change men, and pickpockets—on the show grounds.

But the Ringlings, who valued real family entertainment and had a genuine zest for the circus life, continued to prosper. In 1907 they bought out the Adam Forepaugh & Sells Bros. Circus. The next year they stepped in and saved the Barnum and Bailey Show from certain disaster. They paid $310,000 for the show itself, and another $100,000 for the right to use its slogan: The Greatest Show On Earth. They managed the shows separately for ten years, but in 1918 they made a momentous decision to combine the shows into one enormous circus.

The Ringlings moved the shows out of Baraboo to Bridgeport, Connecticut, changing

Robert Baldwin Collection

P.T. Barnum: Promoter of General Tom Thumb, Swedish singer Jenny Lind, and a giant elephant named Jumbo.

the course of Wisconsin circus history forever. Now the largest of all circuses could begin each season by opening in Madison Square Garden, then touring a host of American cities. Each year, today's Wisconsin residents are reminded of their heritage when the Great Circus Parade wends its way through the streets of Milwaukee. The Circus World Museum in Baraboo keeps the flame of memory burning in Wisconsin, the birthplace of The Greatest Show On Earth.

BADGER PROFILE: Wisconsin's "Bad Boy"

George W. Peck
1840-1916

"Gol darn a turkey anyway! I should think they would make a turkey flat on the back, so he would lay on a greasy platter without skating all around the table. It looks easy to see Pa carve a turkey, but when I speared into the bosom of that turkey, and began to saw on it, the turkey rolled around as though it were on casters, and it was all that I could do to keep it out of Ma's lap. But I rassled with it till I got off enough white meat for Pa and Ma, and dark meat enough for me and I dug out the dressing, but most of it flew into my shirt bosom, 'cause the string that tied up the place where the dressing was concealed about the person of the turkey broke prematurely, and one oyster hit Pa in the eye, and he said I was as awkward as a cross-eyed girl trying to kiss a man with a hare-lip. If I ever get to be the head of a family, I shall carve turkeys with a corn sheller!

—*Peck's Bad Boy At Christmas*

At the age of three, George Peck moved with his parents from New York to settle in the Wisconsin community of Cold Spring. The family later moved to Whitewater, where George learned the printing trade at the *Whitewater Register*. Working on various newspapers from 1855 to 1860, he then purchased half-interest in the *Jefferson County Republican*. Peck stayed for three years, then served with the 4th Wisconsin Volunteer Cavalry in the Civil War.

In 1866, he established the *Ripon Representative*, a newspaper on which he worked for two years before moving to New York City. There he edited the *New York Democrat,* a paper founded by Marcus Pomeroy, an anti-abolitionist who tried to undermine Abraham Lincoln's emancipation efforts through editorials in his publishing effort, the *La Crosse Democrat.* Peck returned to Wisconsin in 1871 to buy that paper from Pomeroy, which he restyled into the *La Crosse Liberal Democrat* the following year. In 1874 he established his own La Crosse paper, *Peck's Sun,* moving it lock, stock, and barrel to Milwaukee in 1878.

In this larger venue, the newspaper became known for its humorous sketches, particularly a series written by Peck, "Peck's Bad Boy." He collected many of these stories and published his best-known book, *Peck's Bad Boy and His Pa,* in 1882.

Peck remained the editor of his paper until elected mayor of Milwaukee in 1890 on the Democratic ticket. His years in the partisan press served him well—he was nominated for governor in that same year, and won the election. He served one term, his main political aim being the shakeup of the Republican Party's firm grip on power in the state. Reapportionment laws passed by his administration were declared unconstitutional, and he was defeated in 1895 by Republican William Upham.

Peck ran unsuccessfully for a second gubernatorial term in the 1904 election, and lived in Milwaukee until his death at the age of 76. It seems that Wisconsin voters appreciated Peck's ability to point out their foibles with a chuckle more than his desire to change their politics.

When they were gone Lulu felt an instant liberation. She thought about the brightness of that Chautauqua scene to which Ina and Dwight had gone. Lulu thought about such gatherings in somewhat the way that a futurist receives the subjects of his art—forms not vague, but heightened to intolerable definiteness, acute color, and always motion—but a factor of all was that Lulu herself was the participant, not the onlooker.

—From *Miss Lulu Bett*

Photo courtesy State Historical Society of Wisconsin

Zona Gale
1874-1938

Zona Gale was the only child of Charles and Eliza Gale of Portage, Wisconsin. Her Scottish father engineered a steam locomotive for the Chicago, Milwaukee and St. Paul Railroad, and her mother, of British descent, graduated from a Madison academy to teach school. They were a close-knit family, and her parents supported her decision to become a writer, a decision made when she was just eight years old.

Zona wrote poems throughout her elementary schooling and into her days at the University of Wisconsin, where she majored in literature. She was the editor of *The Aegis,* the university's magazine, and she wrote her first novel during her senior year. She received her bachelor's degree and worked as a newspaper reporter from 1895 to 1901.

For the first 18 months, Gale worked for Milwaukee's *Evening Wisconsin* as a society writer, then she moved on to the larger *Milwaukee Journal.* She earned her Master of Literature degree in 1899, and she would later receive an honorary doctorate in that field from the University of Wisconsin. In 1901, she moved to New York to work as a reporter for the *Evening World.*

During her reporting years, Gale also wrote romantic fiction and poetry, but had no success in getting it published. By 1903, she left the *Evening World* to pursue a freelance career, and she was soon enjoying success as a writer of serial love stories in magazines. In 1906 her first book of

fiction, *Romance Island,* was published. The previous year, a trip to Portage inspired her to begin writing fiction set in a small, quiet village like her hometown, and her stories about "Friendship Village" were soon appearing in *The Atlantic, Woman's Home Companion,* and other popular magazines. The stories elicited her first real recognition from the reading public, and they were eventually collected in a series of four volumes.

In 1911, Gale won a $2,000 prize from the *Delineator* for her short story "The Ancient Dawn," a less sentimental, more realistic piece of fiction, and she used the money to move back to Portage. After the move, she gradually turned away from the folksy stories of her early years, instead writing gritty, fact-based fiction.

A 1913 meeting with charismatic Senator Robert La Follette led her to endorse progressive Republicanism and to write *Heart's Kindred,* a pacifist-leaning novel. Her friendship with Jane

Addams increased both her pacifism and her zeal for reform. By 1914, she had become director of the American Civic Association, a member of the Women's Trade Union League and the General Federation of Women's Clubs, and vice president of both the Wisconsin Peace Society and the Wisconsin Women Suffrage Association.

One of Gale's novels, *A Daughter of the Morning,* exposed the terrible working conditions endured by women in industry. *Birth* explored the tragedies of small town life, and *Miss Lulu Bett,* a 1920 small-town comedy, went on to become a best-seller. Gale's own dramatization of the book, first performed in 1920, won the Pulitzer Prize for drama the following year.

Subsequently, Gale published six more novels, three anthologies of her short stories, a book of essays, a poetry volume, several plays, and a biog-raphy. By now an avid liberal, she advocated the abolition of capital punishment and censorship, and joined efforts to ensure international peace. She stumped for La Follette and served his Progressive party with enthusiasm.

Gale established a series of creative arts scholar-ships for University of Wisconsin students in 1921, and she also began serving on the Wisconsin Free Library Commission that year. In 1923, she was appointed to a six-year term on the University's Board of Regents.

At 53, she married William Breese and cared for both his 19-year-old daughter, Juliette, and a second, adopted daughter, Leslyn. Zona died of pneumonia ten years later in a Chicago hospital, and was transported home for burial in Portage. Her life was a manifestation of her basic philoso-phy: "Life is more than we can ever know it to be."

Chapter Six

GROWING UP FAST

The energy and ideas of the settlers and their children had transformed Wisconsin from an untamed wilderness into a network of prosperous farms, towns, and cities. New technologies seemed to emerge weekly, changing the way Wisconsin did business.

Thomas Edison's vision of a safe alternative to flammable liquid for lighting and heating had become a reality by the turn of the century. Henry Ford's "Tin Lizzies" were making their noisy way over roads previously trodden only by horses, oxen, cattle, and their owners. Alexander Graham Bell had given us the gift of long-distance communication with his newfangled telephone and, thanks to the daring of the Wright Brothers, we were no longer earthbound in our search for ways to travel farther and faster.

As the world became smaller due to these innovations, unrest in Europe would end America's era of isolationist politics and, in many senses, would steal the country's innocence. The industrial boom also called more and more young people away from the family farm and into the city.

The small town reached its heyday in 1910, when over 17 percent of Americans lived in communities of less than 10,000 people. By 1940, more than half the nation's population was located in metropolitan areas of over 50,000, and a majority of the remainder lived in suburbs. The great influx

Appleton's public works department was obviously quite taken with the newfangled electric light bulb. In 1909, they installed so many on archways that the radiance lent a carnival atmosphere to College Avenue.

Courtesy Marathon County Historical Society

of people into urban areas for work in defense plants during WWII was the final tip of the scale. The passing of the small town was eulogized by Henry Seidel Canby, who edited the *Saturday Review* between 1924 and 1936:

> The town waited for you. It was going to be there when you were ready for it. You belonged, and it was up to your own self to find out how and where. There has been no such certainty in American life since.

Periods of boom and bust played havoc with national economies, plunging many nations, including our own, into a time of deep economic (and psychological) depression. Through it all, Wisconsin's resilient people rose to the challenge of keeping their lives together and making important contributions to their growing state and nation.

City Lights

By 1890, Madison had established itself as a progressive town, due in large part to the presence of the state capitol and the prestigious University of Wisconsin. It sported many municipal improvements that we now take for granted, such as telephones, electric lights, a city waterworks, free home mail delivery, and even a mass transit system of mule-drawn streetcars. As a public service, horse-watering troughs and "bubblers"—hand-pumped drinking fountains—were provided.

Smaller towns such as Stevens Point were beginning to exhibit signs of stability and prosperity as city streets were improved by 1891. Cedar blocks formed the surface of those roads, making the "clop, clop" of horses' hooves and the rumble of wagon wheels more noticeable. As cities were modernized, they generally got louder as well.

Oshkosh had prospered greatly from the lumber boom, and the fortunes amassed by resident timber barons gave it the nickname "Sawdust City." By the early 1900s, it was the world's leading producer of wooden doors and sashes for the building industry.

Courtesy Milwaukee County Public Library

Inter-urban railways extended from southeastern cities and made mass transit possible for residents of surrounding rural areas. Here, however, the East Troy line has collapsed due to the spring thaw, which shifted the track across the swampy "Devil's Teapot" west of Mukwonago in 1917.

Milwaukee became a major center of commerce, fashion, transportation, and communication. By 1875, the volume of lake commerce that passed through its ports and railroad extensions far inland ensured its status as a booming marketplace. It was a leading producer of flour, leather, meat, and (predictably) beer.

Ice was delivered to homes and businesses by horse-drawn wagon, then later by truck. Up to 100 pounds might be delivered to a residence in response to a card placed in the front window, while restaurants and taverns might require several hundred pounds at a time. Ice picks and tongs

Before autos were available, ice and coal were delivered to businesses and residences by horse-drawn wagons such as this one, parked in front of a brewer's regal mansion on Milwaukee's Wisconsin Avenue.

were common household items, used to break up hard blocks that were toted indoors on the shoulders of the burly drivers. Neighborhood children swarmed around the truck while the ice man was making his delivery, stealing shards of the deliciously cold ice and sucking on them as they would popsicles.

In the winter, the same companies delivered wood or coal for heating and cooking purposes. Soot-covered men hauled canvas carriers full of coal to basement windows, through which they shoved metal chutes. The coal was poured into bins, and residents then shoveled it into the furnace.

Smaller businesses used handcarts to deliver their wares and services. Self-employed vendors pushed their carts up and down neighborhood streets and alleys, yelling to reach potential customers. It was common to hear cries of "Rags! Rags!" as the rag man bought worn-out clothes and old newspapers for 15 cents a pound. The junk man patrolled the streets in search of discarded items he could sell as scrap metal, and tinkers stopped to fix broken pots, pans, and kitchen utensils.

A clanging bell told housewives to bring out their knives and scissors for the sharpener, a man who would put an edge on their blades with his well-worn stone. In the spring and fall, a screen and window man came by, offering to install and remove those storms and screens from precarious upper-level windows. He even washed and rinsed them before putting the pieces in storage areas.

Pfeifer & Klecker Meat Market owners and employees pose proudly in front of their neatly kept building, along with the delivery wagon and driver. The turn of the century saw the zenith of family-run businesses, before highly competitive chain stores proliferated and displaced them.

Service With a Smile

As the 19th century came to a close, prosperous towns were filled with small, family-owned shops and stores that proudly offered the finest in goods and services. Almost every business had its own uniform or accoutrements that served to identify the trade of the wearer.

Butchers wore long white coats to catch the blood and fat that spurted from the sides of fresh meat, and their shop floors were covered with sawdust to absorb the same mixture. Coils of sticky, brown flypaper spiraled down from the ceiling, and kielbasa made on the premises hung in great strings in the front windows. In season, the skinned carcasses of rabbits, deer, and other game hung on barrels in front of the shop. Sulze and pickled pig's feet swam in jars, and tripe, brains, and sweetbreads were displayed on open trays. The friendly butcher offered free liver for regular customers' cats, and made suet available for lard rendering.

Barbershops served not only as places for haircuts, but also as social meeting centers for men. The barber himself was a well-kept man dressed in a striped shirt with sleeve bands and maybe an apron. He kept a brush tucked into his rear pocket to sweep tickling hairs off his customers' necks and faces. His shop had one or two foot-pump chairs and other straight-backed chairs for waiting customers or visitors. Men smoked, laughed, and read the requisite *Police Gazette* in an atmosphere heavy with the smells of shampoo, soap, powder, and hair oil.

Drugstores offered a wide variety of medications and household items. Cod liver oil, bromo pepsin, and horehound drops were stocked on shelves with hair nets, bathing caps, gaslight mantles, and fancy boxed stationery. Along with cures for human ailments, you were likely to find animal curatives such as No-Kik Teat Salve, Dr. Robert's Udder Balm, and Genito-Wash for udder hygiene, indicating that the days of the busy family farm were still in full swing.

A favorite institution among children was the corner store, with its glass cases displaying vast, colorful arrays of penny candy. Homemade fudge, long sticks of red and black licorice, sugared green spearmint leaves, and chocolate stars covered with tiny white nonpareils beckoned to the wide-eyed

Stark's Candy Store in Wausau boasted a real soda fountain, a pressed-tin ceiling, tropical palms, and attractive counter girls—everything necessary to draw young men and their dates for turn-of-the-century courting.

This large Milwaukee-area general store was well-stocked in the late 1800s. Whole-bean coffee was stored in the tins at the front of the store, and was custom ground in a huge mill at the rear of the shop. Fresh fruit, in season, was displayed in crates above the coffee, and a sign on the canned goods shelves behind the counter advertises butter for 17 cents a pound.

Excursion boats such as this sternwheeler carried weekend pleasure seekers up rivers and along lakeshores. During the week, they carried commercial freight loads. Here, the steamer Alexander Mitchell takes on passengers for a sight-seeing tour of the Wisconsin Dells.

youngsters. Many spent hours with their small noses pressed against the glass, agonizing over the choice between juice-filled wax bottles and jawbreakers.

In small, family-run grocery stores, the floor was crowded with barrels of soda crackers and huge, plump pickles floating in brine. Fresh fruit and produce, bread displayed in glass counter cases, and whole, boiled hams ready for slicing gave a pungent aroma to the air. Clumps of bananas hung surrounded by fruit flies, and cookies such as almond shorts, Twilight Desserts and fig bars were stacked in glassine-wrapped boxes on a slanted rack. Eggs were stored in cold compartments at the rear of the store, and cereal boxes were retrieved from high shelves with long-handled tongs.

Keeping in Touch

From the earliest days of settlement, staying in contact with families, friends, and the rest of the outside world was important to homesteaders. News from anywhere was prized. It traveled along the verbal grapevine and was often distorted or embellished along the way, but the elaborations were generally admired as fine storytelling. The earliest mode of truly reliable communication was, of course, the mail.

Mail service was established early in the more heavily settled southern part of Wisconsin, but it was not until the mid-1800s that most northern areas were considered civilized enough to support post offices. Mail service was not extended to the Plover portage below Stevens Point until 1842, and there was no official post office in Marathon County until 1850, when Wausau became the northernmost postal station in central Wisconsin.

Eventually, a route was set up between Wausau and the mining town of Ontonagon, Michigan, replacing the steamboats that couldn't run in winter. Originally, a man named Kemp ran the route by dogsled for less than $100 per round trip, but he proved unreliable. After 12 bushel baskets of mail piled up in the spring of 1857, Levi Fleming set out in a canoe with a companion to deliver the mail to

Ontonagon. Fleming's companion mysteriously disappeared at Grandmother Bull Falls during a portage, but Fleming continued on alone. The mail finally reached its destination on June 13th, and Fleming returned to Wausau in early July.

Major southern cities such as Milwaukee, Mineral Point and La Crosse gave rise to many hometown newspapers. Milwaukee had the *Sentinel,* the *Journal,* the *Daily News,* and the *Evening Wisconsin,* among others. La Crosse residents read the *Democrat* and the *Tribune.* Mineral Point offered the *Miner's Free Press* as early as 1838, and many towns published foreign-language papers such as Milwaukee's German *Deutsche*

Zeitung and its Polish *Kuryer Polski,* which catered to the city's large, foreign-born constituencies.

In the early days of journalism, no attempt was made to be objective. Papers firmly espoused the editorial views of their publishers. Stories exhorting the virtues of the Whig, Democrat, and Republican parties and blasting the foibles of their opposition appeared on every page, not only in the editorial section. Many papers were formed for the sole purpose of extending the publisher's political influence.

Newspapers from Chicago and St. Louis sometimes made their way into the "pineries," but when printing presses arrived in northern towns, community

9XM-WHA radio in Madison began broadcasting from this studio in 1917. WHA has the distinction of being the station with the longest record of uninterrupted broadcasting in America. At the time of this photo, the station's broadcasts consisted mainly of Morse code and crackly voice transmission via an unruly tangle of wires, tubes, and bulky transmitters. The hardware was housed in a spare room in the University of Wisconsin's Vilas Hall.

WAAK, Milwaukee's first commercial radio station, broadcast live from this curtained studio in Gimbel's downtown department store. The makeshift microphone at far right was rigged up from a five-cent blotter tied into a tube with string and suspended from a bird cage stand. These four teachers from the Wisconsin College of Music are shown performing in May, 1923, for the station's first broadcast.

newspapers began to appear. As technology improved and telegraphy was introduced, newspapers became more sophisticated by subscribing to the Associated Press wire service. Transcribed in longhand by telegraph operators, current news would appear in the following day's edition, bringing an exciting sense of immediacy to people who had become accustomed to reading about events days or weeks after the fact.

Predictable events such as sporting contests and political elections were covered first on the newspaper's "Play-O-Graph," a board posted outside the newspaper office that displayed translations of AP wire transmissions. People would gather on the street to read a blow-by-blow description of events. If the crowd got too large, a staffer would simply stand in the doorway and shout out the news before posting it.

Telephones came on the scene in the late 1800s. Milwaukee was proud to offer service to 15 customers in 1877, and service in Wausau was limited in 1889 to those who lived within a 20-mile radius from the city limits. As it turns out, that wasn't much of a limitation, since there were few subscribers and therefore few people to call.

In Franksville, 10 to 15 people shared a party line within its Citizen's Telephone Exchange in 1916. For many years, party lines were a source of small-town entertainment for subscribers who eavesdropped on each other's conversations.

The phenomenon of radio debuted in 1917, when 9XM-WHA began broadcasting from Vilas Hall on the University of Wisconsin campus. By 1919, the station was on the air with scheduled broadcasts. It all began with Professor Earle Terry and his

Electric railways were common in larger cities before gasoline-powered buses took over. Their clean power provided efficient—if noisy—mass transit in pleasant surroundings for just a nickel a ride. This Milwaukee car sits in front of the central library building on Eighth Street and Wisconsin Avenue.

students, who built and operated a "wireless telephone" transmitter in 1917. They used it to broadcast telegraph signals first from Science Hall, then radio transmissions from Sterling Hall.

During World War I, other stations were ordered silenced while 9XM remained in operation under a special authorization from the U.S. Navy, to continue its telephonic exchanges with stations on the Great Lakes. Today, WHA is known as the "Oldest Station in the Nation" or, more accurately, as the station with the longest record of uninterrupted broadcasting.

Milwaukee's first radio station, WAAK, transmitted live broadcasts of music and radio theater from Gimbel's department store downtown. Because of the large initial investment, only bigger cities could support their own radio stations. Signals could be received intermittently on AM airwaves from such distant transmitters as Chicago, Detroit, and Pittsburgh, but central Wisconsin had few of its own stations operating until WSAU-AM went on the air in 1937.

To many country folks, the radio was a mystery of newfangled technology that provoked suspicion. They didn't understand how it worked, how to operate it, or how to fix it if it broke. Prior to rural electrification, which didn't become available to most farms until well into the Depression, plug-in sets were useless. Batteries represented an ongoing expense, so most radios existed in the major population centers.

But the lure of the outside world overcame technophobia, and by 1931, the federal census indicated that two of every five homes in the country had a "talking box," and in 1938, it was estimated that over 80 percent of Wisconsin homes had radios, bringing together people of varying economic, geographic, and ethnic backgrounds. People could travel without ever leaving their homes. The world—and the state—seemed to be shrinking.

Getting There

In the earliest days, Wisconsin settlers traveled long distances by water, in canoes and on the stern-wheelers that plied the vast Mississippi and other rivers and lakes. Most steamers near large cities carried commercial freight during the week,

An array of railway passes issued in the 1880s to one William E. Starr, Esq., treasurer of a small Eastern railroad.

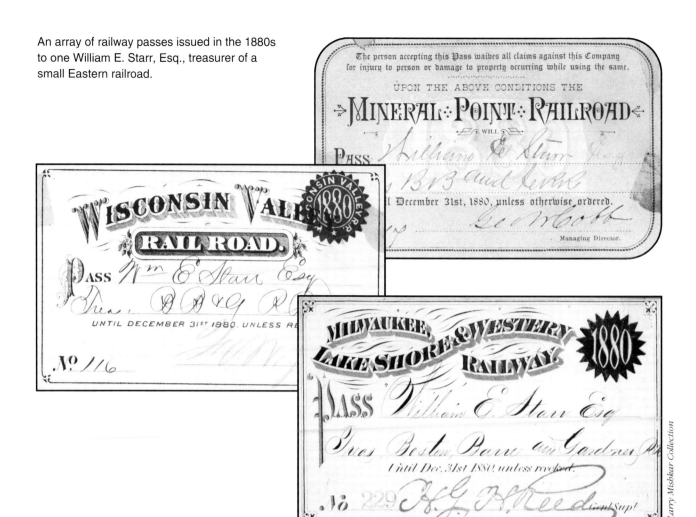

but catered to the excursion trade on weekends. A Berlin, Wisconsin, newspaper described one of these festive outings in 1880:

> One-half the passengers were drunk, three-quarters feeling good, nine-tenths brimming over with fun and frolic, and the whole so jam full of jollification and lager beer that they didn't know which way they were looking.

Railroads entered the picture when the state legislature chartered the first rail line in Wisconsin in 1847. Construction began on the Milwaukee and Waukesha line, which in 1850 changed its name to the Milwaukee and Mississippi. The line reached from Milwaukee to Waukesha in 1851, had extended to Madison by 1854, and crossed the entire state by 1857. Two years earlier another line, the LaCrosse and Milwaukee, had built a connection to Beaver Dam.

During this time, many in state government realized the important role that railroads would play in future transportation and commerce, but the Wisconsin constitution prohibited the state from going into debt to finance internal improvements. It did allow the legislature to authorize cities and counties to buy railroad stock. The localities could then sell stock to individuals, but such bond sales didn't raise enough capital to build a railroad, so the state petitioned Congress for land grants. The 31st and 32nd Congresses refused the request, and it was denied again in 1854, because of pressure from homesteaders who were against making any land unavailable for settlement. They also feared the price increases they believed railroad building would cause.

Byron Kilbourn, the canal-building giant, wasn't about to let his opportunity to make a killing in the railroad business go by the wayside, so he

This train wreck occurred in 1922, two miles west of Chippewa Falls on the Soo Line railway.

spearheaded a huge Congressional lobbying effort. As a result, President Franklin Pierce signed a bill in 1856 that granted over a million acres to Wisconsin for the building of state railroads. A second tract was granted in 1864 to the Wisconsin Central line, part of the same legislative act that got the state's university on its feet. The Wisconsin Central Railway formally organized in Menasha's National Hotel in February of 1871, and located its first office there. Its first train ran from Menasha to Waupaca that September.

Inadequate brakes and signal systems made early rail travel hazardous, but these problems were eventually addressed, and the railroad became one of the most economical means of moving both people and freight. In fact, the rail system became so efficient that it changed the way in which time was kept.

Originally, time was a relative commodity in the U.S. One pundit observed: "Until the 1880s, all time throughout the country was local time; when a clock in Madison said 11:10, it was 11:16 in Milwaukee and 11:17 in Chicago." In other words, there was no true standard time.

In November of 1883, to aid in the regulation of route schedules, railroads adopted what was called "Standard Time." From then on, correct time could be obtained at a railway station when the signal came over the telegraph wire. The federal government, never quick to jump on practical matters, didn't recognize standard time zones until 1918, when they were adopted by the Bureau of Weights and Measures.

In 1873, the Reverend Dr. J. W. Carhart of Racine designed and operated the first self-propelled highway vehicle, which he called "the Spark." Powered by a two-cylinder steam engine, it was steered with a lever and had a top speed of five miles per hour. Without benefit of liquid fuel, rubber tires, or ball bearings, the Spark was a noisy contraption. Despite its shortcomings, however, it was revolutionary enough to earn its inventor the title "Father of Automobiles" at the 1908 International Automobile Exposition in Paris.

A chauffeur stands beside this Rambler in jaunty driving coat, gloves, cap, and goggles. The car is parked in front of Wausau's Third Street courthouse in 1905. The Rambler was manufactured by the Thomas Jeffrey Company of Kenosha.

The first internal combustion automobile ever purchased in the United States was produced in 1895 by A.W. Ballard, an Oshkosh bicycle maker who built automobiles as a sideline. Karl Benz and Gottlieb Daimler had been building autos in Germany for the previous decade, but Henry Ford hadn't yet gotten around to introducing his famous assembly-line plants. The state's first mass-produced auto was the Rambler, assembled in Kenosha by the Thomas Jeffrey Company, also a former bicycle manufacturing business.

The automobile soon took on a sophisticated mystique in American life. Everyone had to have one. Running boards on the sides of cars were popular for use as picnic serving areas and places to have one's picture taken. The custom of taking a leisurely Sunday drive became so prevalent in the years before the First World War that the government later had to restrict the practice to conserve gas for the war effort.

With increased travel came the need for better roads. Previously, horses and small buggies could be maneuvered around muddy areas, but the new "horseless carriages" were susceptible to becoming mired in the large puddles and mudholes of unpaved roads. Plank roads were seen as the answer to this dilemma.

Modeled after the earlier "corduroy" roads made of logs laid side-by-side, plank roads were built by laying 4x4 oak stringers on leveled grades. Across them, eight-foot planks two to three inches thick were spiked in place. These roads were built by private investors, and drivers paid tolls that were collected every five or six miles. Only one of the many plank roads built in this manner was financially successful. Eventually, these roads were replaced by others paved with macadam or concrete.

In 1917, Wisconsin introduced use of the highway marking system that we now take for granted. For the first time, numbers were used to designate highways. North-south roads were given odd numbers and highways with a primarily east-west orientation were even-numbered. The system was eventually adopted by the Federal Highway Control Board, and is now employed throughout the nation.

At about the time autos were beginning to dominate the roads, William Harley and his associates Arthur, Walter, and William Davidson began working on a motorized bicycle in a backyard shed on the outskirts of Milwaukee. They sold their first machine in 1903. Two years later, they were turning them out at a rate of about ten per year.

This farmer shows off his new "Silent Gray Fellow," an early model Harley-Davidson motorcycle named for its quiet operation and understated paint job. Motorcycles were a welcome revolution in travel, combining the best features of automobiles and bicycles, and Harley-Davidson became the standard by which all other American-made models are judged.

Nicknamed "Silent Gray Fellows" for their quiet operation and subtle paint job, the early Harley Davidson motorcycles bore little resemblance to the flashy, roaring vehicles of today.

Appleton put the state's first commercially viable electric street railway into service in mid-August of 1886. The cars ran along tracks imbedded in the streets. They were powered by direct-current motors, which were themselves driven by hydro-electric generators. The current was conducted through two trolley wires strung above the tracks, and a metal conducting pole connected the car to the wires. These electric streetcars became common in major metropolitan areas, usually operated by electric light companies seeking to maximize return on the investment they'd already made by wiring the various neighborhoods.

Only seven years after Orville and Wilbur Wright's historic Kitty Hawk venture, experimental attempts at self-powered flight were being undertaken in Wausau and, in 1913, the first discussion about building a municipal airport was held. Although the idea was rejected at the time, it was shelved for future consideration. An airport was in fact built in 1921, and the facility was taken over by the city in 1926. Airmail service came in the late '30s, and many World War II pilots received their flight training at Wausau. The Kenosha airport also served as a training ground for WWII pilots by conducting a "Flying Cadets" program.

The first actual flight in Wisconsin took place in Beloit in November, 1909. Flight engineer Glen Curtiss designed and assembled a biplane there, which was piloted by Arthur P. Warner. With that

Famous aviator Amelia Earhart addressed the Central Wisconsin Teacher's Association in October of 1936, praising the advantages of air travel.

his automotive inventions, which included the automobile speedometer.

Flight came to Milwaukee County in 1919, when the Park Commission established Currie Park as the first airport. It was one of the earliest publicly owned airfields. The nation's first commercial air transport took off from Currie Field in August of that year, a month after inauguration of the airport. The demonstration flight went to New York City and Washington, D.C. It was a Lawson Airliner, a two-engine biplane with a 95-foot wingspan. The craft carried 16 passengers and two pilots, and it returned to Currie Park on November 15th.

The first Milwaukee airmail flight also took off from Currie, in June of 1926. The field was deactivated that November—a month after the county had purchased Hamilton Field, a 163-acre tract of farmland south of Milwaukee proper, near Lake Michigan.

flight, Warner became the eleventh American to fly a powered aircraft and the first in the country to use it for business purposes. Warner taught himself to fly, and used aircraft to research and publicize

A Hamilton single-engine airplane, manufactured in Milwaukee, sits in front of the terminal at the county's first airport, Currie Park, in the late 1920s.

Milwaukee County Airport was relocated to Hamilton Field in 1927, in its present location south of the city near Lake Michigan. The terminal building in this photo was replaced in 1940 by a larger structure erected by WPA workers. The facility was renamed General Mitchell Field in 1941.

The new field was named for its founder, Thomas Hamilton, a local aviator who ran a propeller-manufacturing business. The Milwaukee County Airport started out as a single wooden hangar, but within nine months the first terminal building was opened in a farm house that still stood on the property. A few days later, on July 5, 1927, the first scheduled airline passenger service was established by Northwest Airways, which carried passengers in three Stenson biplanes.

A two-story brick terminal with a centrally located control tower was soon built to replace the farm house, and the brick structure was itself replaced in 1940. The new terminal building was erected by the county's Works Progress Administration at a cost of $177,000. In March of 1941, the airport was renamed General Mitchell Field in honor of General Billy Mitchell, a Milwaukee native who advocated use of air power in the struggle for battlefield supremacy.

The Great Depression

The Allied victory in World War I and the subsequent economic boom produced a euphoria among Americans that came to a screeching halt when the stock market crashed on October 29, 1929. Businesses went bankrupt at an alarming rate, and others were forced to lay off or dismiss workers. People who were still working were forced to take drastic pay cuts. In the absence of a social safety net, millions of people found themselves out of work and unable to pay their bills. Many lost their homes and businesses.

Agricultural families were hit particularly hard. Since the boom years had mostly benefited industrial businesses, farmers hadn't fully shared in the prosperity, and most were already on less than solid ground. Faced with heavy debts and recurring drought, they saw the market for their products collapse, since there was little money available.

By the beginning of 1932, day laborers on Wisconsin farms, who usually performed only short-term jobs such as repair work or milking, were paid an average of 80 cents per day plus board, or $1.15 without board. Monthly workers, who were employed on longer-term tasks such as planting or threshing, made a monthly average of $12.74 with board or $24.00 without. The figures represented a 59 percent decrease from wages prevalent just two years earlier.

City people were willing to work on farms in return for food. But the farm families themselves were in a bad way. Children scavenged through pig scraps to find something to eat. Mothers made children's clothing out of feed and flour sacks. Some kids never saw their first store-bought pair of shoes until they entered high school.

In the worst years, farmers sold whatever they could, at a loss if necessary, just to hold onto their farms. Cows sold for as little as a penny per pound, eggs for nine cents per dozen. Overall farm prices dropped as much as 57 percent, paralleling the shrinking of wages. In Wisconsin, dairy farmers were the hardest hit, and the Milk Strikes of the 1930s, staged to protest price fixing by the Milk Board, were some of the most violent of the era. Angry producers dumped cans of milk on roads and train tracks to underscore their unwillingness to sell to a market that was taking advantage of them. Some farmers, crossing picket lines due to fear of losing their farms, were dragged from their wagons and beaten, their cargoes ravaged.

Many farmers lost everything when mortgages were called in by banks that were also trying to stay afloat. Some resisted the taking of their farms with violence, attacking lawyers, auctioneers, and bank officers who had arrived to sell their property. At times, large crowds of frightened farmers gathered to threaten auctioneers, and sheriff's deputies were often called in to keep the peace with tear gas.

Verna Maassen writes of one such farm sale in her story "The Penny Auction," part of a collection of stories entitled *We Were Children Then* (Stanton & Lee). She describes how a family farm was saved in 1934 by neighbors who refused to pay any reasonable amount for the items being auctioned off:

> The auctioneer had set up the sales ring and the clerk's table on one side of the big oak tree. On the other side lay a coil of three-quarter-inch hay rope. The crowd stared at the rope, remembering the threatened hanging of a reluctant judge in Iowa who had refused to accept proceeds of a penny auction.

> The first horse went up. The auctioneer boomed "What am I offered? Come now, spring work's just beginning."

Courtesy Milwaukee County Historical Society

This "Hooverville" —the name given shantytowns that sprang up all over the country in the wake of mass evictions—emerged along the Lincoln Park riverway in Milwaukee, after many people lost their homes because local banks called in the mortgages. The shantytown was washed away by spring floods in 1931.

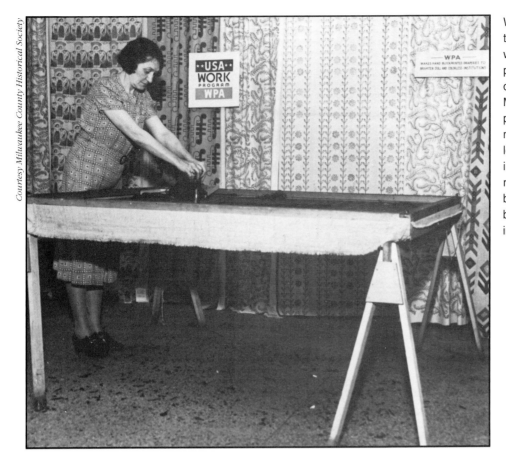

Works Progress Administration (WPA) projects were instituted to put people back to work all over America. Here, a Milwaukee woman screenprints textiles that would be made into draperies for local government buildings. A notice on the wall reads, "WPA makes hand blockprinted draperies to brighten dull and colorless institutions."

A man reached down, picked up one end of the hay rope, coiled it into a noose, then threw it contemptuously to the ground.

"Twenty cents!" came from one side.

On and on the auction went. The best cows for twenty-five cents. The poorer ones for fifteen and twenty cents. Pigs for five and eight cents. A plow for one dollar. A grain binder for two dollars. The "10-20 tractor" for five dollars.

The sale was ended. The auction sales clerk paid the proceeds of the sale to the bank officials, legally satisfying the mortgage. Then the auctioneer and the clerk, the bank officials and the moneyed people got into their cars and drove swiftly out of the yard. One by one, the neighbors led the stock they had bought back into the barn.

Rural families weren't the only ones affected. In the early Depression years, a shantytown sprang up along Lincoln Park riverway in Milwaukee, housing people who had lost their homes when collapsing banks had called in the mortgages. Spring floods washed the "community" away in 1931.

Among the city's residents was a large Communist contingent that moved in to take advantage of the civil unrest caused by the Depression. During huge rallies in Haymarket Square, political rabble-rousers would harangue crowds of unemployed workers. In the winter of 1930, 57 people were arrested in Milwaukee in a "labor riot" staged by a mob of unemployed people demanding work from city government. Many labor unions became militant, using sit-down strikes and similar methods around city hall to demand more jobs.

Desperation was everywhere. One Kenosha worker told the Wisconsin Legislative Interim Committee on Unemployment in 1931:

I am a laboring man through and through. I raised a family of nine children. Two of them are working a half day a week over to Nash Motors. And I am about to lose my home. I

In 1930, Milwaukee endured a strike by employees of the Chicago and Northwestern Railroad. Violent labor clashes characterized the times throughout Wisconsin.

had it twenty-seven years. Haven't worked for two years. Who is going to do anything for me? My children can't help me. They can't even pay their board.

Local governments did what they could, abandoning use of earth-moving machinery to opt for manpower. They hired men with picks and shovels to build highways, maximizing the number of men they could put to work. It wasn't until Franklin Roosevelt's New Deal, however, that things began to look up.

The New Deal generated Works Progress Administration (WPA) projects statewide. In Milwaukee, a book-binding project was established utilizing the large number of local workers trained in the printing industry. Artists painted murals in government buildings such as post offices and libraries. Hospitals and sanitariums were renovated and redecorated, as were city halls and county jails. Fire protection was improved through the building of cisterns and reservoirs, and municipal tennis courts, playgrounds, parks, and swimming pools were constructed. School grounds were repaired or added in many communities. Athletic parks and stadiums were erected, and youth activity buildings were raised.

In Milwaukee, one of the biggest boosts to manufacturing was provided by the repeal of the

Volstead Act—when 3.2 beer was pronounced non-intoxicating in 1933, 85 brewery workers were rehired.

Named for its sponsor, Minnesota Representative Andrew Volstead, the 1919 act upheld the 18th Amendment to the U.S. Constitution, which prohibited the sale, manufacture, and transportation of all alcoholic beverages. Most people simply referred to it as "Prohibition."

Prohibition Jolts a Brewing Economy

Prohibition did much to harm heavily German-populated towns, where brewing was a major source of economic strength, and the onset of the Depression only aggravated an already unstable situation. Some breweries tried to offset the blow by turning their energies to manufacturing other products. Schlitz Brewing Company turned out candy bars and baking chocolate under the name Eline. One company on Milwaukee's south side turned ostensibly to the production of potato chips, but only a portion of the raw potatoes were being used for that product. Strange odors coming from the factory led inspectors to discover that many of the potatoes were being turned into mash and allowed to ferment into a bootleg whiskey that vastly outsold the potato chips. After avoiding serious reprimands several times, the factory was closed down.

Federal raids weren't the only dangers faced by illicit moonshiners. The volatility of the distilling process also put boot-leggers at risk. Here, bystanders gawk at the wreckage caused when a clandestine still exploded in Cudahy in 1932.

These non-teetotalers, undaunted by newsreels showing the consequences of illegal drinking, felt safe enough in the seclusion of Wisconsin's northwoods to flaunt their disdain for Prohibition.

As might be expected, Prohibition only increased the attraction of alcohol for adventurous souls, and moderation was discouraged. Since any sale of alcohol was illegal, many vendors began breaking other taboos such as selling to minors. Alcohol-producing stills proliferated in many city cellars and on farms. "Near beer" was made up in kitchen sinks to the accompaniment of accordion music and dancing in the basement on Saturday night. A popular song of the era featured these honest lyrics: "Everybody's feelin' bad 'cause liquor must go/But you can always get yourself a little Old Crow."

"Blind pigs"—illegal taverns disguised as farm houses—and roadhouses abounded in rural areas,

"speakeasies" in the cities. Flappers and their young men in raccoon coats or broad-lapeled zoot suits danced the fox trot and the Charleston, and met outside for a swig from the hip flask.

Even the newsreels in theaters, which showed Federal agents shooting and axing beer kegs in Chicago in an effort to keep Al Capone and his gang from rum-running, failed to discourage the black market in alcoholic beverages. When Congress, realizing the futility of trying to legislate non-consumption, repealed the amendment in 1933, the reaction was immediate and widespread. The news was greeted by dancing in the streets, the blaring of car horns, and pubs that sprung open and stayed open all night.

A U.S. Deputy Marshal and his assistant destroy a cargo of illegal beer seized in a raid on Milwaukee's Amherstberg Corporation in 1930.

Some notorious personalities found the relative isolation of northern Wisconsin ideal for the operation of bootlegging activities. This is the main lodge built on Cranberry Lake (near Couderay) by Chicago mobster Al Capone. His private pontoon planes would fly to the location with cargoes of "hooch," land on the lake, and loaded trucks would then distribute the moonshine. Another northwoods location, Little Bohemia in Manitowish Waters, was a rendezvous site used by John Dillinger's gang when the action` down south got too hot. It was the scene of a shootout with the FBI in 1934.

Civilian Conservation Corps

Two aspects of the Depression era that dramatically affected Wisconsin were the rural electrification program and the Civilian Conservation Corps.

Proponents of Franklin D. Roosevelt's "New Deal" recognized that economic growth could not occur in areas that were without the modern amenities provided by electricity. The Rural Electrification Administration offered funds for the construction of transformer stations, administered by cooperative programs in outlying areas. This federal agency, created by Franklin D. Roosevelt in May of 1935, was continued by an act of Congress on May 20, 1936. The program not only put people to work, it allowed them to modernize farming operations that had been laboring under inefficient methods.

A farm on U.S. Highway 14 near Richland Center was the first in Wisconsin to obtain central station electric power from a rural cooperative. Constructed in 1917 by a man named James Harold, the farm was wired for electricity in anticipation of the provision of power not too far in the future. On January 8, 1936, the Richland Cooperative Electric Association energized the first section of its network, and the farm was connected in May of the following year.

The Civilian Conservation Corps was formed in 1933, administered by the government as one of the first New Deal programs. It recruited unemployed young men between the ages of 18 and 25 from across the nation, including the territories of Puerto Rico, the Virgin Islands, Hawaii, and Alaska to work on projects

Courtesy Roland R. Applin

These CCC enlistees are working on the construction of a dam for a new trout rearing pond on the Deerskin River near Argonne. Heavy machinery was eschewed in favor of manpower, in order to provide work for as many men as possible.

The Rib Mountain Lookout in 1938. The CCC would transform Rib Mountain into one of the state's most popular tourist attractions.

received the remaining $5. This ensured that the money provided to fund the project was going to the targeted beneficiaries, since 25 percent of the heads of households were unemployed and still needed to raise their families. The wages kept many families together until the Depression eased.

Men working on rural projects lived in barracks, and were assigned to quasi-military units. They built roads, parks, trout-rearing ponds, and useful structures. They planted trees on state, county, and federal lands— nearly three billion nationwide, 265 million in Wisconsin alone. Timber stand improvement, construction of parks, roads and fire lanes, lake and stream surveys and improvements were all activities performed by CCC enrollees. They also performed erosion control measures (an especially important job during the Dust Bowl years), put up telephone lines, and participated in the erection of rural electrification transmission networks.

Men involved in urban CCC improvements were housed in Army-issue tents with room for eight cots. The enrollees kept their personal items in a "barracks bag" hung inside. Meals were also Army-issue, such as reconstituted eggs and black coffee. The workers wore the standard-issue uniform of khaki shirt and pants, work boots, and khaki "monkey jackets." Green ponchos kept the rain out, and black ties were issued for formal dress occasions.

In his book, *Growing Up The Hard Way in the 30s,* Harold Gauer recalled his CCC experiences in Company 650 just outside of Milwaukee. The year was 1933:

> Camp Gilmanton personnel wore U.S.
> Army fatigues and clodhopper shoes and

intended to improve the country's crumbling roads, buildings, and public areas.

The recruits enlisted for a six-month hitch, and could voluntarily reenlist following that period. Most recruits re-upped at the end of their first tour, for lack of available work in the private sector. Generally, the young men who participated were single and came from needy families. Food, shelter, clothing, and medical care for corps members were supplied by the military, so all the men had to worry about was performing their assigned duties.

The main thrust of the program was to provide the young men with the dignity of honest work and the hope that comes from being able to feed one's family. The nation benefited because the CCC workers restored long-neglected resources and infrastructure.

Wages were $30 per month, of which $25 was sent directly to the man's family. The enrollee

Retreat.
Camp Pine River (F-8 Wis.)
Three Lakes, Wis.

Photo
Spencer & Wyckoff
Detroit

R.

CCC members assemble in front of their barracks at Camp Pine River near Three Lakes. Camps were maintained in quasi-military fashion.

bounced out in the back of a truck with shovels and axes to deal with farmland erosion. They did that by constructing concrete retaining dams across gullies the county surveyor indicated could be saved from eroding further. That meant hammering together a lot of boards to make forms, anointing them with oil, laying and tying together reinforcement rods, and arranging to flush slops of concrete down sluices.

Forty-five thousand camps provided meaningful, useful work for three to four million men in the hardest-hit areas of the nation. Fifty-four of these camps were located in Wisconsin, employing 66,155 men. Funding for the program was terminated in 1942 after the nation's entry into World War II, and many of the CCC alumni stepped right back into uniform to engage in that conflict.

One hundred twenty-eight Wisconsin worksites were activated during the nine years of the CCC's existence, and evidence of its accomplishments is today visible in the trail networks of our state and county forest lands, state parks, national forests, and campgrounds.

One of Wisconsin's most popular tourist attractions, Rib Mountain State Park, is successful today because of work performed by 250 members of the CCC. The workers improved access to the park, installed ski facilities and built a shelter house, transforming the site into the most popular winter sports attraction in central Wisconsin.

The Wisconsin Civilian Conservation Corps Museum is located in Rhinelander, and stands as a tribute to those who participated in one of the most successful of the New Deal programs.

BADGER PROFILE: Bringing Wisconsin to Life

Edna Ferber

1885-1968

Selina was a farm woman now, nearing thirty. The work rode her as it had ridden Maartje Pool. Faded overalls, a shirt, socks, a boy's drawers grotesquely patched and mended, towels of rough sacking.

She, too, rose at four, snatched up shapeless garments, invested herself with them, seized her great coil of fine cloudy hair, twisted it into a utilitarian knob, and skewered it with a hairpin from which the varnish had long departed, leaving it a dull gray; thrust her slim feet into shapeless shoes, dabbed her face with cold water, hurried to the kitchen stove. The work was always at her heels, its breath hot on her neck.

—From *So Big*

Edna Ferber was born in Kalamazoo, Michigan. She and her family followed her father, Jacob, to a series of midwestern towns where he established dry goods and general stores. Edna's mother, Julia, was a strong woman from a spirited Chicago family. When her husband's health and vision failed, she took over his business, called "My Store," on Appleton's College Avenue. In Appleton, Edna attended Ryan High School and wrote for the school newspaper.

Ferber had her heart set on studying for a career as a stage actress. When her mother informed her that family finances simply wouldn't allow it, Edna rushed in tears to the offices of the local newspaper, *The Crescent,* where she convinced the editor to name her Appleton's first girl reporter. She received the handsome salary of $3 per week. The young reporter attacked her job with zeal, covering stories about the Poor Farm, behind-the-scenes action in the Barnum and Bailey Circus, and even managing to garner an interview with screen actress Lillian Russell.

A year and a half later, a new city editor was hired at *The Crescent.* An old-fashioned newspaperman, he was unaccustomed to women in the office and promptly fired Edna. Crushed, she began combing the state for other opportunities. The *Milwaukee Journal* put her to work as a legal reporter. In later years, Edna would look back on her four years at the *Journal* as her "college education." Still feeling the sting of her first firing, she was overzealous to prove herself worthy, and fainted one day while getting dressed for work. Suffering from exhaustion and anemia, she went to her mother's Appleton home to recuperate.

Ferber acquired a second-hand typewriter and began writing her first novel, *Dawn O'Hara,* based on her experiences in Milwaukee. She sold her first short story and a second, and decided not to return to newspaper life, determined instead to make her living by writing fiction. Ferber finished *Dawn O'Hara,* but could find no magazine willing to serialize it.

Her father died during this time, and Edna's mother sold the store to move with her girls to Chicago. While packing for the move, Edna almost tossed the manuscript of her novel into the furnace, but her mother advised her against such rash action. Instead, Edna sent it off to the agent who had helped Zona Gale get her work published. By the time Edna arrived in Chicago, her book had been accepted for publication.

Ferber continued to write fiction based on her Wisconsin experiences. *Come and Get It* recalled the Fox River Valley lumberjacks, and her description of Appleton farm families carries the story in *So Big*. Her tenure at the *Appleton Crescent* provided grist for the story of a small-town news-paper in *Cimarron,* and she fondly recalled her high school days in *A Peculiar Treasure.*

Ferber's first series of short stories, based on the life of newswoman Emma McChesney, introduced the American businesswoman to fiction in 1910, and started the author on her road to fame and fortune. Later, Ethel Barrymore starred as Emma McChesney in a theatrical production of one of Ferber's books.

Ferber went on to write six plays with famed playwright George S. Kaufman, including *Dinner at Eight* and *Stage Door.* Many of her books became Hollywood films, including *Show Boat, Cimarron,* and *Giant.* When she died at the age of 82, Edna Ferber left behind 12 novels, 11 volumes of short stories, six major plays, and two autobiographies. Her prolific life helped bring Wisconsin to life in the imaginations of readers and on the silver screen.

BADGER PROFILE: A Pioneer in Photography

Henry Hamilton Bennett came to Kilbourn City (now Wisconsin Dells) from his native Quebec in 1857. He served with the Union Army during the Civil War, and returned to the Dells in 1865 to purchase a photographic business.

As a photographer, he originated methods for trimming, washing, printing, and mounting pictures, and devised improvements for his cameras. He built a jack for his camera so it could be raised or lowered to achieve just the right angle—a feature incorporated into modern tripods. He also changed over to the new "wet " development process that replaced the direct "Daguerrotype" with negatives and prints, invented by English photographer W. H. Fox Talbot. However, he was not an astute businessman, and his photo studio failed.

Bennett moved to Tomah with his wife in 1867, where he worked for a time out of a tent. That winter, he returned once again to the Dells and re-opened his studio. He developed a brisk trade in stereoscopic scenic views of the natural beauty of the area. Never satisfied with existing technology, he pushed his equipment to its limits. By setting his camera on a windowsill during a storm with its shutter open, he captured one of the first filmed images of lightning. Using the same technique, he later created some of the first photos of fireworks.

Bennett developed a fast shutter that could freeze movement in fractions of a second. Using this high-speed photography, he became a major landscape photographer, traveling the scenic Dells area in a boat equipped with its own darkroom. He captured swirling waters, reflections, and logging rafts going over dams—things the public had never

Photo courtesy State Historical Society of Wisconsin

H.H. Bennett

1843-1908

before seen on film, though we now take such "freeze-frame" images for granted.

Two of Bennett's inventions, the solar enlarger and the revolving printing house, were restored by the Smithsonian Institution in 1978, and are now on display in the National Museum of History and Technology. His former studio still stands, open to the public as a Dells attraction, and it's the oldest photographic studio in America. It was placed on the National Register of Historic Places in 1976. The studio and its contents are maintained by the H.H. Bennett Studio Foundation, with the purpose of keeping his photographic legacy alive.

This captivating view of Lone Rock, taken in 1885 from below the Lower Dells, is typical of H.H. Bennett's pioneering work in scenic photography. His innovative shutter techniques allowed him to retain sharp, static images while capturing the movement of clouds and water to evoke a sense of nature for the viewer.

Hail to Our Soldiers

GRATEFULLY INSCRIBED TO

...Our Brave and Fearless Boys...

. . . BY . . .

Will L. Pfefferkorn

AUTHOR OF " SUNSET ON THE RIVER."

PUBLISHED BY

547 TWENTY-SEVENTH ST.   ...A. H. HAMMETTER...   MILWAUKEE, WISCONSIN.

This is the cover of a piece of sheet music composed by Milwaukeean Will Pfefferkorn in honor of the Union soldiers who fought Confederate troops in the Civil War.

Chapter Seven

PULLING TOGETHER

Wisconsin was initially affected less by the outcome of the 1860 elections than many states in the Union. With the exception of a few outspoken abolitionists, the state had little direct stake in the slavery issue, because its economy wasn't affected and because most of the settlers were new immigrants. Slavery was not, for them, a burning issue. Some found the practice morally repugnant, but these were a minority.

The Civil War

Things began to change when several southern states seceded from the Union upon learning of the presidential victory of Abraham Lincoln, a Republican from Illinois with abolitionist sympathies. There was no formal military conscription at that time, so each state decided for itself how to react. Shortly thereafter, the Wisconsin Democratic Party met in convention and decided that the Union must be preserved at all costs. By that time, the Civil War was already underway, and there was little else the convention could do.

When Wisconsin's troops began marching to battle, they distinguished themselves as soldiers of the first order. Colonel Hans Heg, a Norwegian-born immigrant, led the Fifteenth Wisconsin regiment into many battles in the South. His horse

Union soldiers return triumphantly from battle to march down the main streets of Milwaukee in a September, 1865, parade.

Courtesy Milwaukee County Public Library

Old Abe

Perhaps the most colorful story of Wisconsin's service in the Civil War is that of Old Abe, the eagle mascot of the Eighth Wisconsin regiment. The eagle was born in 1861 on the north fork of the Flambeau River, six miles north of present-day Park Falls. Two young Chippewa Indians captured the eagle chick and traded it to Dan McCann, a Chippewa Falls trading post operator, for a bushel of corn. When the war began McCann, who was disabled, felt his family should be represented in the fight, and volunteered his eagle to Commander John Perkins of Company C of the Eighth Wisconsin in Eau Claire.

Soldiers named the eagle Old Abe, in honor of their president. Legend has it when Company C marched through the gates of Camp Randall to join the rest of the Eighth regiment, Old Abe flew from his perch, caught the corner of the flag with his beak, and held the Stars and Stripes out to its full length with his wings flapping. From that day forward, the Eighth was known as the Eagle Regiment, and on that memorable day Old Abe was sworn in along with the rest of the regiment.

After heading south in October of 1861, the Eagle Regiment first engaged and subdued the Confederate troops led by General Jeff Thompson. They fought again at Island No. 10 and New Madrid, Missouri, in the spring of 1862. That May, they fought the Rebels at Farmington and in Corinth, Mississippi. The following October, the Confederates tried to recapture Corinth, an important supply line link.

Confederate General Price wanted to recapture the town, but he also had a second objective: to kill or capture Old Abe. So great was the morale boost provided Union troops by the bird's presence that Price swore he'd rather capture "that damned Yankee buzzard" than an entire brigade of Union troops.

Concentrating their attack on the Eagle Regiment, the Confederate soldiers charged northern positions. The outnumbered Eighth was reluctantly giving ground to the enemy until cries of "There's Old Abe!" rang out up and down the battle line. The eagle was soaring in spirals above enemy troops, screaming his defiance of their attack. Emboldened by the antics of their mascot, the Eighth rallied, routing the Confederates.

In the next two years, Old Abe participated in 36 more battles, and Union troops believed that his presence guaranteed victory. He was twice hit by enemy fire, but was never seriously wounded. He returned in 1864 to Wisconsin with remnants of the Eagle Regiment whose enlistment was up. The men refused many offers to buy the bird, including a $20,000 offer from P.T. Barnum, who wanted to use the eagle as part of his circus act. Instead, they presented him to the governor as an honored resident of the capitol.

The esteemed eagle made appearances at political and fund-raising functions all over the country until a fire swept through the capitol building in 1881. The building was saved when Old Abe's cries alerted guards, but America's first combat aviator died of smoke inhalation. In 1941, the U.S. Army's 101st Airborne Division proudly carried an eagle mascot to war, appropriately named Young Abe in honor of its predecessor.

Old Abe was a bald eagle carried into battle for three years by the 8th Wisconsin Infantry during the War Between the States. This photo, taken about 1875, served as a model for the eagle monument that still stands in Vicksburg, Virginia.

was shot out from under him at the battle of Stone's River, Tennessee. He survived to lead his men into bloody combat at Chickamauga, Georgia. There, he was struck in the leg by a minié ball from a sharpshooter's musket. Heg continued to ride, leading his men until he was unable to stay in the saddle. He died the next morning at 33 years of age, and his statue stands on Madison's capitol grounds.

Another person who distinguished herself in service to her country was Cordelia Harvey, the "Wisconsin Angel." After touring the unsanitary field hospitals of the South, she petitioned President Lincoln to set up army hospitals in the North, which would be easier to keep clean and functional. Lincoln feared that soldiers recuperating from their wounds in the North would desert as soon as they were able to walk. Mrs. Harvey countered his concern with the observation that, "Dead men cannot fight and they may not desert. If you permit them to come North, you will have ten

men where you now have one." Lincoln was persuaded.

Mrs. Harvey set up hospitals in Milwaukee, Prairie du Chien, and Madison, where her medical unit was named for her husband Louis, who had drowned near Savannah, Tennessee, in 1862. Here, soldiers could forget about the war for a time as they recovered from their wounds in the clean and cheerful hospitals of the North. Hundreds who would otherwise have died in filthy field units at the front lived to fight again.

A World at War

As the tumult of the Depression waned and New Deal programs slowly put the nation back to work, people began to look forward again to the future. Behind them lay the uncertainty of the Civil War and the pain and suffering of the First World War.

The latter conflict had touched Wisconsin at its very heart, dividing the loyalties of its predominantly German settlements. In Milwaukee, as the U.S. entered the "war to end all wars," a mob forced an end to German dramas at the Pabst Theater; the Brumder Building's German statue was hidden away from those who would deface it; and German businessmen who didn't buy Liberty Bonds found placards on their doors questioning their loyalty to America.

Despite these ugly events, people managed to maintain a sense of humor and their love of good entertainment. Player pianos could be heard accompanying such war-inspired songs as "If The Rest Of The World Don't Want You, Then Go Back To Your Mother And Dad," "And He'd Say Oo-La-La, Oui, Oui," and "If He Can Fight Like He Can Love, Then Good Night, Germany."

But the years of innocence and isolation were coming to an end. The treaty of Versailles left Germany broken and embittered. Twenty years later, Germans thought they had found a savior in Adolph Hitler and the fevered patriotism he inspired. The black cloud of Nazi imperialism rolled over western Europe as country after country fell

Milwaukee native Erwin Wehlitz poses in uniform during World War I. His "boot camp" is Camp Hancock in Augusta, Georgia.

Ration Books were issued at irregular intervals to U.S. citizens. They contained ration stamps for use in buying staples such as meat, oil, dairy goods and fuel, which were in short supply during World War II.

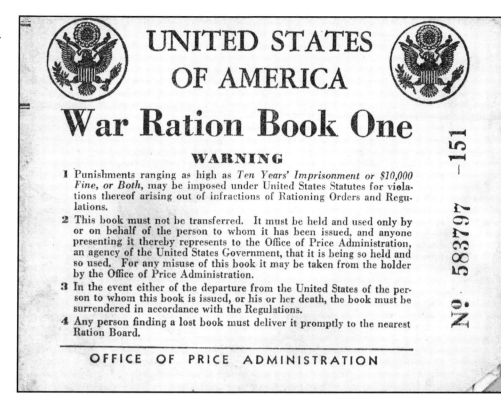

UNITED STATES
OF AMERICA

War Ration Book One

WARNING

1 Punishments ranging as high as *Ten Years' Imprisonment or $10,000 Fine, or Both,* may be imposed under United States Statutes for violations thereof arising out of infractions of Rationing Orders and Regulations.

2 This book must not be transferred. It must be held and used only by or on behalf of the person to whom it has been issued, and anyone presenting it thereby represents to the Office of Price Administration, an agency of the United States Government, that it is being so held and so used. For any misuse of this book it may be taken from the holder by the Office of Price Administration.

3 In the event either of the departure from the United States of the person to whom this book is issued, or his or her death, the book must be surrendered in accordance with the Regulations.

4 Any person finding a lost book must deliver it promptly to the nearest Ration Board.

OFFICE OF PRICE ADMINISTRATION

No. 583797 −151

Larry Mishkar Collection

before the onslaught of Hitler's storm troopers and the powerful Panzer divisions.

Wisconsin's heavy equipment manufacturers were already contracting to provide supplies for Roosevelt's Lend-Lease Act, passed to help Britain defend itself against the German blitzkreig. Wisconsinites and Americans throughout the United States found themselves trading a decade of impoverished, uneasy peace for a booming economy built on war.

The Big One

Families just home from church and perhaps enjoying a leisurely lunch stopped in their tracks on December 7, 1941. Junior put down the Sunday funnies and Dad turned up the volume when the radio broadcast of the Chicago Bears vs. Chicago Cardinals football game was interrupted by the terrible news of Japan's surprise attack on Hawaii's Pearl Harbor naval base.

Despite the continued influence of "Fightin' Bob" La Follette's pacifist politics, Wisconsin jumped into the fray with as much enthusiasm as any state when war was officially declared. Manufacturing

switched from consumer goods to producing wartime supplies. The industrial port cities—Milwaukee, Kenosha, and Manitowoc—kicked into high gear, mobilizing their work forces into round-the-clock shifts to achieve maximum production. Fort McCoy and other training camps that had lain dormant for almost 20 years sprang to life with new military recruits and volunteers.

On the home front, rationing went into effect to conserve badly needed essentials. Posters exhorted the public to buy defense bonds that would help finance the high cost of making war. One featured a handsome pilot gazing at the viewer and saying: "You Buy 'Em, We'll Fly 'Em!" By the end of the war, Wisconsin had topped 150 percent of its bond quota, and Milwaukee held the honor of being the top bond-buying city in the nation. Bond rallies replaced dances as the new social event, unless you happened to be a USO volunteer, in which case you nearly made a career of learning all the latest dance steps so you could entertain servicemen on leave.

Country life changed as the boys left for duty overseas and women handled the farm chores. But because of Wisconsin's position as a leading agricultural state and dairy producer, farm life here changed less than elsewhere. Jerry Berard, a young dairy and hog farmer in the township of Wausau, was the only son able to assist in the running of the farm. He was given an agricultural deferment and remained at home during the war years. In an interview for a special booklet published by the Marathon County Historical Society, he asserts:

> I thought, "Yes, I would like to go into the service." My objective was to be a fighter pilot. I passed my military physical in Milwaukee. A lot of my friends and buddies were drafted, and I wanted to get in and do something good, too. According to the government, though, they wanted farmers to produce [for the war]. There were going to be shortages of sugar and meat and all that. I guess the government made the decision that I should stay on the farm.

Excitement in the City

The real change came in the cities. Heavy equipment manufacturers there were clamoring for workers on every shift, and people poured in from all parts of the country to answer that clarion call. Many were still suffering the after-effects of the Depression-era unemployment, and were only too happy to fill the wartime positions.

J. I Case became a leading manufacturer of military parts, equipment, and armaments for the American effort in World War II. These two workers—true "Rosie the Riveters"—in the Racine plant are shown assembling a medium-sized rib for the wing of a B26-C bomber (also known as the Martin Marauder). Other items that Case manufactured included airplane nose cones, tail cones, after coolers, and the "airborne tractor," a modified farm implement designed to be flown into action and used for construction of roads.

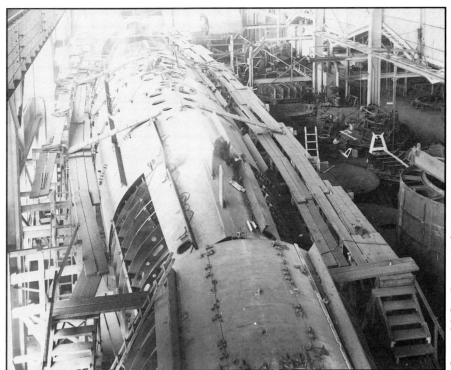

J.I. Case manufactured 155mm shells used by Allied troops in World War II. The shells were completed on this line in the finishing room, and the first one was delivered to the War Department on August 4, 1941. Each finished shell weighed nearly 78 pounds, measured a little over six inches in diameter, and stood almost two feet high.

Governor Julius Heil formed the 12-member Wisconsin Council of National Defense, with representatives from agriculture, commerce, industry, labor, and government. This distinguished panel was to advise the governor on the best use of the state's resources in the war effort. Dane County was one of two in the nation selected as a test site to determine the practical value of collecting aluminum—essentially, the nation's first aluminum recycling program.

Labor and industry worked together to arrive at the most efficient means of getting supplies manufactured and to the front, resulting in the largest increase in hiring since 1914. Nearly twice the number of wage earners were employed during 1941 as in the Depression year of 1932. About 75 percent of that increase occurred in metalworking industries with government armament contracts. With increased overtime hours at the overtime pay rate, the average weekly wage for factory workers in the state was $31.77 in 1941, compared to $15.61 in 1932.

With the decrease in production of consumer goods, there were layoffs in non-defense-related industries, but those workers were quickly absorbed into defense plants. Before America entered the war, about 200 Wisconsin firms were involved in primary defense contracts, a number that increased exponentially in the following years. Among the Wisconsin companies producing material for military use were:

- Allis-Chalmers, Milwaukee—airplane materials;
- American Brass, Kenosha—cartridge discs;
- A.O. Smith, Milwaukee—bomb bodies;
- Briggs & Stratton, Milwaukee—fuses;
- Chain Belt, Milwaukee—howitzers;
- Giddings & Lewis, Fond du Lac—machine tools;
- Gisholt Machine Co., Madison—machine tools;
- Harley-Davidson, Milwaukee—motorcycles;
- Heil Company, Milwaukee—trailers, trucks, pumps, etc.;
- J.I. Case Company, Racine—forgings, bomber parts, shells;
- Kearney & Trecker, Milwaukee—machine tools;
- Kohler Company, Kohler—fuses and shells;
- Oil Gear Company, Milwaukee—hydraulic mechanisms.

Smaller industries in Wisconsin contributed woolen uniforms, raincoats, blankets, underwear, gloves, socks, shoes, aluminum mess kits, guns, and food. According to the Wisconsin Blue Book for 1941,

The hull shop at Manitowoc Shipyards is shown during World War II. Very few workers are visible in the photo, due to the tight security maintained throughout the war. Critical manufacturing processes were not revealed.

farmers increased their milk production by eight percent in the first year of the war (about four times the national average), hog production was up ten percent, and vegetable harvests were up 33 percent.

For the first time, women entered the work force in large numbers to replace men who had gone off to fight, a development that profoundly shook up the American social order. Women were paid less than men, and often endured scorn, ridicule, or harassment from men who couldn't get used to having women in the workplace. In 1943, Rosella Wartner of Wausau was earning 38 cents an hour working at Marathon Battery, packing batteries into waterproof cases for shipment overseas, to be used in Army flashlights, bazookas, and field radios. Ms. Wartner recalled a factory experience with the government inspector who toured the plant daily:

> He was a ladies' man, and I didn't like that. One day he stood straight behind me and he'd always be breathing down your neck. He always stood so close.

I'd be hanged if I'd put up with that! So I watched for my chance. One day he stood behind me and I took one step back and I stepped on his toes. And I wore shoes with heels on! I just stepped down real hard. He never stood behind me anymore!

In 1942, Milwaukee's Falk Corporation allocated $50,000 to the construction of washrooms for "possible women employees." Their foresight paid off, since by 1943 over 500 females worked in the plant, and the number was growing.

Heroes in an Unlikely Place

One extraordinary contribution to the war effort was made by Manitowoc, a port city with a proud heritage of shipbuilding that dated back to the days of the Great Lakes schooners. In this unlikely harbor, 28 of the submarines used in World War II were built. Named for various real and imaginary marine creatures, the ships were considered the best in the world at the time. Three hundred and eleven feet long, each sub carried a crew of eight officers and 72 enlisted men, along with a payload of 24 torpedoes.

In order to transport the submarines from the upper western shores of Lake Michigan to their destinations around the world, Manitowoc Shipbuilding invented an ingenious floating drydock that allowed subs to be lifted out of the water over unnavigable river stretches. At Manitowoc, the subs were loaded onto this drydock, floated down the lakeshore to Chicago and onto the Chicago River, from there to the Mississippi River, and on into the Gulf of Mexico. The ability to perform this transport clinched the contract for the Manitowoc firm.

Contract work on the submarines peaked in 1940, when over 7,000 workers were employed in their manufacture. The *USS Peto* was the first sub completed, launched at Christmastime in 1942. Launchings became cause for great celebration, and entertainment was provided by such Hollywood notables as Abbott and Costello and Spencer Tracy. Afterward, everyone retired to the nearby Elks club for dancing.

The *Peto* was followed a month later by the *Pogy*,

and during 1943 nine of the big ships left Manitowoc. The *USS Guavina* was the first to be turned out in 1944, followed by nine more during that year. In 1945, the *USS Lizzardfish* led the way for six other subs, culminating in the launch of the *Mero* in November of that year. Manitowoc Shipbuilding was also responsible for the production of 37 LCT-5 landing-craft troop carriers and ten Navy oil tankers used during the war.

The company produced its own shipyard employee publication called *The Keel Block*, which was used as a morale-builder and served to give employees a voice in the company. The shipyard was featured in the May 18, 1942, issue of *LIFE* magazine, and again in the January 11, 1943, issue of *TIME*. An example of the "Gato" class of submarines built in Manitowoc, the *USS Cobia,* is today moored at the community's Maritime Museum, and is available for public tours.

On the Homefront

People who had been unemployed got jobs during the war, and those who had been working for a while generally moved up a notch as men left for the European and Pacific fronts. Just plain jobs, so

Courtesy Manitowoc Maritime Museum Archives

The *U.S.S. Peto* rolls into the water in Manitowoc at Christmastime, 1942. It was the first of 28 submarines launched by the Manitowoc Shipbuilding yard.

scarce only a few years earlier, were no longer desirable. Everyone wanted a position in the defense industries, to feel they were "doing their part." Others with less honorable intentions sought jobs that were considered work "in the national interest" to avoid finding draft notices in the mail—particularly after deferrals for marriage and fatherhood were no longer valid.

Prices shot up as the nation prospered, even with strict price controls in place. Havana cigars went up to 15 cents, and a plate lunch that formerly cost 35 cents was now half a dollar. Smokers were disappointed to find that many of their favorite brands of cigarettes had "gone to war," leaving them with such also-rans as Black and Whites and Dominos. "Victory Trucks" made the rounds of school playgrounds to collect every kind of mate-

rial, from cooking fats and aluminum pots and pans to old radiators and golf clubs—anything that could be used in the production of ammunition and armaments.

Gasoline, sugar, meat, coffee, and silk hosiery were rationed through the use of cards and stamps. New appliances, automobiles, and other consumer goods were unavailable to all but the most essential war workers "for the duration." Shortages were rampant. For one Milwaukee woman, going to work in the office at Allen-Bradley's foundry and metalworks without nylons was the worst part. "We had to stand in line for nylons in the stores," she recalls. Nylons replaced silk hosiery when silk was remanded by the government to make parachutes.

Racine's 1943 Goodwill Fourth of July parade held special significance for J.I. Case workers, who knew their own handiwork was contributing directly to the war effort. The parade featured a float demonstrating the building of B-26 bomber wings.

A Milwakee scrap metal drive resulted in this collection of items, here being sorted for processing into World War II armaments and equipment.

Fashion reflected the impact of the war, including "Eisenhower" suits (short-waisted to mirror the military cut) for women and cuffless pants for men (to conserve on fabric). A *Milwaukee Journal* advertisement from the era touted lipstick available in "Patriot Red," a shade that promised to glorify the wearer's lips with "exciting beauty."

Wall posters in public places reminded Americans that "Loose Lips Sink Ships," a dark inference that the world was rife with potential spies. Security, especially around defense plants, was at an all-time high, sometimes carried to absurd extremes. A Brokaw woman whose job required her to inspect small torpedo components recalls her experience in a Virginia Navy production facility:

We did all top-secret work at the factory, so when I went home at night I couldn't even tell [my husband] Michael what I did. Every time a rumor would come out from the factory, we were all frisked the next day by a Marine guard, and most of the employees were women.

To this day, she isn't sure which parts of the torpedo she was inspecting.

Hollywood churned out miles of patriotic footage, serving the war effort as an arm of the government propaganda machine. After a full-course meal for under $1 per person, families in 1942 could choose between more than 70 Milwaukee area theaters, with over 80 titles offered for 15 to 30 cents a seat. Usually, the price bought a double feature

Rationing of Gasoline, Fuel Oil, Canned Fruits and Vegetables Is Called Off Today

GREEN BAY PRESS-GAZETTE

26 PAGES · GAZETTE ESTABLISHED IN FEBRUARY, 1865 · FREE PRESS ESTABLISHED IN MAY, 1814 · GREEN BAY, WIS., WEDNESDAY EVENING, AUGUST 15, 1945 · ASSOCIATED PRESS UNITED PRESS · PRICE 5c

PEACE COMES TO WORLD

Huge Crowds Orderly As City Celebrates

Seven Injured, None Seriously, In Turnout Marking Peace Announcement; Holiday for All Sees Stores, Industries and Offices Closed

Continue Meat, Butter Rations

OPA Limitations Upon Other Commodities to Rule for Time Being

U.S. Military Machine Rolls to Victory Halt

Jap Cabinet Members Quit; One a Suicide

Allied Commanders Move To End Hostilities and Stop Further Bloodshed at Once

This headline celebrated the Allied victory in World War II, and signalled the imminent return of Wisconsin's servicemen and women.

---

preceded by a cartoon, a film short, previews of coming attractions, and a newsreel.

Cinema-goers tired of war dramas might have opted for George Montgomery in *Riders of the Purple Sage,* or Paulette Goddard and Bob Hope in *Nothing But The Truth.* Musicals were also popular, their huge casts and flamboyant productions just the thing to take a person's mind off the grim realities of war.

Popular songs on the Hit Parade included "Don't Sit Under The Apple Tree With Anyone Else But Me" and "When The Lights Go On Again All Over The World." Swing tunes by such orchestras as Count Basie and big band sounds like Glenn Miller's war-inspired "Boogie Woogie Bugle Boy" were favorites on the dance floor.

The importance of professional sports was downplayed as many star players entered military

service, sometimes replaced by minor league rookies, "4-Fs," or women's leagues. Nevertheless, Milwaukeeans crowded into dilapidated Borchert Field to see the minor league Brewers play some baseball and win three consecutive championships by 1942. College and school teams also provided much-needed diversion.

By the end of the war, one-ninth of the state's population—332,000 men and women—had entered the service, most of them going overseas. Of the enlisted population, 7,980 were killed, and thousands more were wounded. When a family lost one of its members, one of the blue stars on the window flags turned gold. Wisconsinites, like Americans elsewhere, became war-weary and disillusioned. The promise of a swift and glorious victory had evaporated in the face of a bloody conflict that dragged on for nearly five years.

On VJ day in 1945, factory whistles blew. Church

and school bells rang. The Fruit Growers' Cooperative cannery in Sturgeon Bay tied down the lever on the whistle and blew it until the steam ran out, and an effigy of Japanese prime minister Tojo was dragged through the streets behind a car. Madison's capitol square swarmed with cheering masses.

Ashland citizens hung a likeness of Japanese emperor Hirohito from a 15-foot scaffold, soaked it in gasoline, and torched it. Racine's downtown ornamental pools were filled with over 300 citizens who were giving each other "victory dunkings." Ration cards were torn up and used for confetti in an impromptu victory parade in Oshkosh. Milwaukee residents yelled for joy and swarmed into the streets, halting traffic as they hugged, kissed, or danced with the nearest available person. Some wept with joy at the end of the longest struggle they had ever known.

In Wisconsin, in the United States of America, and in all of the allied countries, people had pulled together and won the war, but the world had changed forever. It was the end of an era, for Wisconsin and the world. Just around the corner, in 1948, Wisconsin would also mark the end of its first century of statehood.

BADGER PROFILE: Prairie-Style Architect

Frank Lloyd Wright

1869-1958

In 1869, a genius was born in Richland Center. Frank Lloyd Wright later enjoyed a happy boyhood in Spring Green and, in 1884, entered the University of Wisconsin to study civil engineering. After receiving his degree, he moved to Oak Park, Illinois (a western suburb of Chicago), married, and fathered six children.

A restless and unconventional man, Wright rejected commissions for new buildings there, took a mistress, Mamah Borthwick Cheney, and moved back to Spring Green in 1911. On this, his mother's land, Wright built a new home and named it "Taliesin." The structure wholly embodied his developing aesthetic of architecture, an aesthetic that resulted from Wright's exposure to Joseph Silsbee's midwestern shingle style, existing midwestern architecture, and traditional Japanese design. Mirroring the midwestern prairie landscape, Taliesin displayed an emphasis on horizontal roof lines, graduated building heights, and an unpredictable placement of porches.

Wright believed strongly in emphasizing a oneness with the land. He found an artificiality in the accepted practices of civil engineering that offended his sensibilities. In an interview late in his life, Wright expounded on what he felt was an appalling lack of sensitivity among city planners:

> We have created ugly cities because of the pig-piling instincts we inherited from our savage ancestors. The caveman huddled to keep warm. He huddled for protection against beasts. There's no reason for us to keep pig-piling, but we do it. We even pass pig-piling zoning laws. They force a worker to live so far from his work that he is in transit more hours than he works.

Wright's strong views resulted in the formulation of his "Bill of Wright's For The Wage Earner":

1. The right to work safely for a fair wage.

2. The right to live close to his job.

3. The right to beauty at work and in his home surroundings.

4. The right to produce a product in which he can take pride.

In 1932, Wright began operating an architectural training school out of Taliesin during the summer, moving it to Arizona's Paradise Valley in the winter months. His "Prairie Style," with its ground-hugging appearance, overhanging roofs, walled gardens, terraces, and open floor plans caught on regionally among high-profile clients and middle-class families as well. Soon, Wright's reputation as a daring, maverick designer assumed global proportions. After his Tokyo Imperial Hotel withstood an earthquake in 1923, he was hailed as a giant of world architecture.

The headquarters of the Johnson Wax Company, designed by Wisconsin's most illustrious architect and completed in 1939.

Courtesy S.C. Johnson & Son, Inc.

However, Wright's prairie style, designed for family living, never caught on among tastemakers worldwide, and his residential designs remained a minor national phenomenon. They are found predominantly in Spring Green, Madison, and Milwaukee within Wisconsin, in the Chicago area, and in Phoenix, Arizona.

Wright's flamboyant, unconventional career ended with his death at 89, and a horse-drawn grain wagon carried his remains back to his resting place at Taliesin. His work enjoys periodic revivals of interest and continues to influence commercial architectural theory and design.

Photo courtesy State Historical Society of Wisconsin

Jessie Jack Hooper

1865-1934

War will not end war. No matter who wins, everybody loses. Millions of men may be killed, nations bankrupted. War is entirely emotional. It is insanity. Public opinion is the most powerful weapon the world has today to end war. We must provide the machinery for the settlement of international problems by peaceful means. It is a personal, individual responsibility.

—From a 1928 speech

While visiting her married sister in Oshkosh, Jessie Annette Jack met young attorney Ben Hooper. They married in 1888, when Jessie was 23. The couple settled in Oshkosh and had a daughter.

In the 1890s, Jessie established the first kindergarten and the first visiting nurse program in Oshkosh, and she helped found a sanitarium for tuberculosis sufferers in Winnebago County. A staunch Progressive, she joined many clubs and civic service organizations. She occasionally lobbied for reform in the state legislature, asking that the age of legal consent be raised for girls,

seeking to protect women and children in industry, and advocating welfare measures.

In 1893, she was moved to work for women's suffrage when she heard a speech delivered by Susan B. Anthony during the World's Columbian Exposition in Chicago. From the beginning of their marriage, her husband had voted on alternate election years for the candidates of her choice, and he supported her when she decided to join the Wisconsin Women Suffrage Association in 1900. Hooper worked for the organization for almost 20 years, then moved to the national level, lobbying in Washington for a federal suffrage amendment. Her work following Congress' adoption in 1919 of the 19th amendment, which granted women the right to vote, helped ensure that Wisconsin was the first state to ratify it.

Hooper's stature was recognized by her election in 1920 as the first president of the League of Women Voters, but she resigned after serving only two years, in order to accept the Democratic nomination for the U.S. Senate. She knew she probably wouldn't defeat vastly popular incumbent Robert La Follette, but she believed that women were now duty-bound to accept such opportunities. She was also interested in furthering her newest interest, world peace, and believed her candidacy could do so.

A passionate and eloquent speaker, Hooper continued to work on behalf of world peace. In 1932, she was one of the women from many countries who presented the League of Nations with peace petitions carrying over eight million signatures. Her health was failing, in part due to her overwhelming political schedule, and she died in 1934. She was 70 years old.

Jessie Jack Hooper could have followed accepted patterns and chosen a life of leisure. Instead, she recognized the injustices of a world afflicted by a severe imbalance of power, and chose to pour her energies into changing that world.

If you enjoyed
Wisconsin: The Way We Were,
be sure to ask for these fine
NorthWord/Heartland Press titles:

The Land Remembers Collector's Edition by Ben Logan. The best book ever written about family and farm life is now illustrated with lavish contemporary photographs of Wisconsin farm country, plus never-before-published photographs from the author's family album.

Cafe Wisconsin by Joanne Raetz Stuttgen. For the fan of homestyle cooking, here is the guide to over 170 of the finest and friendliest small-town cafes in Wisconsin—plus stories of the cafe owners, the regular clientele, and the towns themselves.

Wild Wisconsin by Brent Haglund. A photographic journey through Wisconsin's most beautiful natural areas. With 51 state parks, 14,900 lakes, 2,000 miles of hiking trails, and over three million acres of public lands, Wisconsin is one of the "wildest" states in the nation.

The River Is Us by Bill Stokes. A collection of thoughtful, down-to-earth essays by the popular nature columnist for the *Chicago Tribune*—who actually lives in Madison, Wisconsin.

Guide to Wisconsin Outdoors by Jim Umhoefer. Descriptions, maps and photos of Wisconsin's outdoor recreation opportunities, including 70 state parks, nearly 2 million acres of state forest, important canoe routes, and wildlife refuges.

Haunted Wisconsin by Beth Scott and Michael Norman. More than 60 tales of ghosts, apparitions, and supernatural occurrences in Wisconsin.

Published by NorthWord Press, Inc.
P.O. Box 1360
Minocqua, WI 54548

For a free color catalog of NorthWord products, call 1-800-336-5666.